Making Morality

Making Morality

PRAGMATIST RECONSTRUCTION
IN ETHICAL THEORY

Todd Lekan

Vanderbilt University Press • NASHVILLE

This book is printed on acid-free paper.
Manufactured in the United States of America

Library of Congress Cataloging-in-Publication Data

Lekan, Todd, 1967–
    Making morality : pragmatist reconstruction in ethical
theory / Todd Lekan.— 1st ed. p. cm. — (The Vanderbilt library
of American philosophy) Includes bibliographical references and
index.
ISBN 0-8265-1420-0 (alk. paper)
ISBN 0-8265-1421-9 (pbk. : alk. paper)
    1. Ethics. 2. Pragmatism. 3. Dewey, John, 1859-1952.
    I. Title. II. Series.
BJ1031 .L45 2002
171'.2—dc21
                                        2002014987

for Vivian

Contents

Acknowledgments

This book owes much to the insightful criticism of Hugh LaFollette, who subjected an early version of this manuscript to thoughtful, honest, and detailed criticism. Michael Eldridge offered many useful comments, especially with regard to the final chapters. Jennifer Welchman provided sharp criticism of the first chapter. Although she may not agree with the final result, I hope that I have managed to do some justice to her concerns. Members of the Midwest Pragmatist Study Group in Chicago heard a version of the first chapter. I cherish many discussions with group members including, among others, Charlene and Hans Seigfried, Bill Myers, Gary Herstein, and Ken Stikkers. My exposure to the work of the late Frederick L. Will while doing graduate study at the University of Illinois had an important impact on my thinking about pragmatism. Although I only had a few occasions to interact with Will in person, I owe a great debt to him. James D. Wallace's philosophical work, seminar in moral philosophy at the University of Illinois, and sage advice were critical sources of insight to which I remain indebted. Richard Schacht, Allen Hance, and Bert Koegler provided valuable help during the writing of the dissertation that began the gestation of the ideas in this book. Robert Kraut's seminar on Richard Rorty and Bernie Rosen's survey course on pragmatism sparked an abiding interest in pragmatism while I was working on my master's degree at Ohio State. I am grateful to both. John Lachs and Cornelis

DeWaal provided critical advice that helped bring this book to completion. I thank copyeditor George Roupe and the staff of Vanderbilt University Press for their great work in the editing and production process.

I wish to thank the Philosophy Documentation Center, publisher of *International Philosophical Quarterly,* for permission to use parts of my article "The Normative Force of Genealogy in Ethics," which originally appeared in volume 23, no. 145 (March 1997), in Chapter 5.

My wife, Vivian Wagner, has continually challenged me to rethink what my philosophical practice means. For her honesty and shared commitment—and for the title of this book—I thank her. My children, William and Rose, four and two at the time of this writing, continue to teach me about shared learning. I thank them.

Introduction:
Pragmatic Metaethics as Revisionism

This book defends a pragmatist account of morality. By "pragmatist" I mean an account of morality that builds on the work of the classical pragmatist tradition of American philosophy and in particular, Dewey's contribution to that tradition.[1] What I find most important in the pragmatist philosophical tradition is the claim that *practice is primary*. This focus on practice is radical—more radical than perhaps has been realized. It is not just the idea that philosophy should be applied to practical questions like how to build better schools, how to make our economy more just, or how to treat dying patients. Without a doubt, pragmatists maintain that philosophers have a vocational obligation to be involved in the problems of their community, forging conceptual tools that will help shed light on its problems. But the pragmatist proposes something more fundamental than the application of theoretical concerns to practical problems. Pragmatism challenges our very conception of theorizing, since it views theorizing as an intrinsic feature of practical activity.[2] The choice, for pragmatism, is not between theory and practice but between intelligent and unintelligent practice. To say that philosophers should be concerned with intelligent practice is to reject the very assumptions that make a radical break between "theory" and "practice." Pragmatism is committed to the idea that philosophical views of rationality, human nature, morality, knowledge, and metaphysics need to be interpreted as theoretical tools that arise out of our need to make practices more intelligent. Pragmatism is a revisionist philosophy. Pragmatism criticizes both philosophy and common sense insofar as these tend to mask the transient and contingent sources of our conceptual interpretations of reality. Our anxieties about human finitude and contingency lead us to project higher unchanging realities, be these God, the forms, the moral law, or the world as it is "in itself." Instead of using our conceptual creations to manage the precarious realities around us, we hide from the precarious by projecting realms of perfect being that exist far from where we are now.

Why do we project these ideal realms? We humans are rational and imaginative animals. Rational speculation frees us from the immediate and enables us to project plans, concepts, and ideals that help us to understand and control our world. However, human reason often distorts its own activities. Our power of imagination idealizes our contingent lives in ways that lead us to suppress awareness of our contingent origins. We construct stories about otherworldly salvation or ultimate immutable truth that tend to distort the fact that we are intelligent animals living in a perilous world.[3]

With respect to morality in particular, we might offer similar compensatory explanations of the idea that moral principles or rules reflect a changeless reality of moral truth. One explanation might appeal to social ideology. Political and religious authorities and members of dominant groups maintain their power by appealing to unchangeable, transhistorical truths to which they are privy. Some of our everyday commonsense morality appeals to transhistorical moral truth in order to legitimate the role of such dominant powers. For example, religious conservatives in the contemporary United States appeal to unchanging biblical truth to maintain the legitimacy of heterosexual marital unions and the moral wrongness of homosexual marital unions. The common understanding of marital morality is based on unchanging sexual mores that favor heterosexuals. The idea that moral principles are unchanging and fixed helps maintain the privilege of those who benefit from adherence to those principles. There are also psychological "benefits" in believing that moral principles reflect an unchanging order of moral truth (although ultimately, these prove inadequate for long-term resolution of problems). The painful tragedies that mark human life provide incentive to hide behind the veil of timeless moral truth, where all goods are realized and no sacrifices need be made.

Within modern moral philosophy—especially modern metaethics—we find some tendency to abstract from actual commitments and practices. Philosophers use the human power of theoretical and imaginative speculation to abstract from our experience as–participants in moral practice. For example, philosophers ask, "Are moral properties genuine properties in the world?" The answer can only come from the very perspective external to the contingent practices from which the question arises in the first place. Once you conceive of a moral property as an attribute of an object "out there" that is observable from God's perspective, then whether or not you affirm or deny the existence of such properties you have taken up a perspective on morality that is external to the practices within which moral considerations are used, discussed, revised, defended, or rejected.[4] Pragmatism is a *reconstructive revisionism* of moral beliefs. It corrects theoretical and commonsense interpretations of morality by being dead serious about rather ordinary features of practical life whose implications are often passed over by common sense and philosophical speculation. I will return to this point shortly.

The Roots of Ethical Theorizing

Since pragmatists take seriously the primacy of practice, they must be careful to give an adequate account of how their metaethical theorizing relates to practice. One way to do this is to be extremely self-conscious about what Dewey calls the *principle of selective emphasis.* This principle is meant to apply to all domains of human thought and inquiry. It says that all theorizing involves making choices about what sorts of data, hypotheses, and principles are relevant for the specific purposes of particular inquiries. Dewey complains that the problem with much philosophical theorizing is that it denies, or at least does not avow, the fact that it has made such a selection for special purposes of special inquiries. Failure to avow such choice usually involves falsely taking one's abstractions to be the whole of the reality from which the abstraction has come. Of this principle Dewey writes,

> Selective emphasis, choice, is inevitable whenever reflection occurs. This is not an evil. Deception comes only when the presence and operation of choice is concealed, disguised, denied. Empirical method finds and points to the operation of choice as it does to any other event. Thus it protects us from conversion of eventual functions into antecedent existence: a conversion that may be said to be *the* philosophical fallacy, whether it be performed in behalf of mathematical subsistences, esthetic essences, the purely physical order of nature, or God. . . . The pursuance of an empirical method is . . . the only way to secure execution of candid intent. Whatever enters into choice, determining its need and giving it guidance, an empirical method frankly indicates what it is for; and the fact of choice, with its working and consequences, an empirical method points out with equal openness.[5]

In this passage Dewey points out that one prominent fallacy that arises from denying choice is "converting eventual functions into antecedent existence." What this might mean in the case of moral inquiry is taking theoretical abstractions such as "principles," "values," or "obligations" to be practice-independent realities that are mirrored in our theories. The pragmatist advises us to view moral concepts as theoretical tools developed out of efforts to resolve problems in our practices. Thus, moral theory that adheres to the principle of selective emphasis will take great care to acknowledge that its theoretical abstractions derive from practice and ,ideally, ought to function to help make practices more intelligent.

Following Dewey, let's try some initial conceptualizing of morality and moral theory according to the principle of selective emphasis. Dewey's hypothesis is that moral theory is simply a more systematic reflection of what we must do when different customs, practices, and activities with their unique goods come into conflict. The origin of such moral reflection can be traced in the development of an individual or an entire community. Of the origin of moral theory in the individual, Dewey writes, "No fundamental difference exists between systematic moral theory . . . and the reflection an individual engages in when he attempts to find general principles which shall direct and justify his conduct. Moral theory begins, in germ, when one asks "Why should I act thus and not otherwise? Why is this right and that wrong?"[6] Dewey then notes that "moral theory cannot emerge when there is positive belief as to what is right and what is wrong, for then there is no occasion for reflection. It emerges when men are confronted with situations in which different desires promise opposed goods and in which incompatible courses of action seem to be morally justified."[7] This need for moral theory is found not just in individual thought and action but also "when a whole community or group in a community finds itself in the presence of new issues which its old customs do not adequately meet."[8] This account of the origin of moral theory leads to the view that its function is to guide the reconstruction of cultural practices, customs, and activities. Thus the whole apparatus of moral theory —including its ideals, values, principles, rights—should be understood as a set of theoretical tools that result, more or less deliberately, from efforts to understand and resolve problems in our practices.

The Plan of the Book

In this book I argue that what Dewey calls "habits" and Frederick Will refers to as "norms" are the most fundamental theoretical tools in pragmatist moral theory. Following Dewey, I take "habits" to refer to socially shared ways of thinking, feeling, and doing that reside in evolving activities and practices. Not to be thought of as mechanical rote responses, habits are dynamic response patterns that help to focus behavior and attention. A habit may reside in many practices and activities. Its character and meaning can only be determined in light of its role in an activity or practice and in its connections to other habits.

The book begins by exploring practical knowledge in ordinary intentional activity and in practical justification through the lens of Deweyan habits. I demonstrate that, notwithstanding its innocuous ring, the claim that fixed ends function as explanations and justifications of actions can in fact distort important features of practical life, such as the rational change of ends and the relation between practical knowledge and will.

By accepting the view that habits are central for any adequate account of practical reason, I argue that the moral domain is defined by those habits that involve responsibilities for relationships. This account of morality navigates between radical particularism and universalism. Its principles are generalizations from prior cases that regulate our learning about new cases.

I use this view of moral domain to defend the idea that good moral arguments are concerned with interpretations of the meanings of norm-governed activities that express responsibilities. Commitment to good moral argument is itself a higher-order responsibility. The book concludes by applying this view of moral argument to social criticism. I argue that good social criticism is local and undertaken by the engaged critic. Good social critics make a community conscious of its responsibilities by interpreting its shared meanings and values in the context of democratic social practices and institutions.

I do not offer a complete pragmatist moral theory in this book. Rather, my efforts are limited to providing pragmatist answers to the following questions: What is the structure of practical reason in intentional action and justification? What is the relationship between practical reason and values? What is the proper understanding and function of moral principles? What distinguishes moral from nonmoral norms? What is the best account of social criticism? Reaching a clear understanding of these questions is an important task in its own right. Deweyan pragmatism suggests a distinct account of the nature of moral theory and practical reason that has not yet been given serious consideration in contemporary metaethics.

Yet we should keep in mind that the idea of a "complete" pragmatist moral theory is a misnomer. Pragmatists view theories as tools devised to grapple with specific problems. Theories, like other human inventions, evolve through history. The tools that I offer in this book should be supplemented with others, including a worked-out value theory, pragmatist analysis of specific moral problems, and the development of a cooperative inquiry between moral philosophy and other sciences.[9]

Reconstructive Revisionism

Pragmatism involves revising commonsense accounts of morality in order to draw radical implications from rather "ordinary" observations about human life. As Hugh LaFollette aptly puts it, "pragmatism is at once both familiar and radical. Familiar in that it begins with rather ordinary views; radical in that it often sees in those views insights that philosophers and lay people miss or misunderstand."[10] Thus, my pragmatic interpretation of morality as habits that involve responsibilities for relationships is based in part on commonplace observations such as the fact that a human can only be moral by acquiring habits in shared practices. Yet it also makes proposals that appear revisionist when measured against ordinary understandings—for example, the claim that moral considerations are essentially *only* modifiable learned ways developed contingently over time to solve particular problems that are in many respects no different in kind than practical considerations in activities like hunting, baseball, medicine, and painting.

It must be noted that there are different sorts of philosophical revisionism. A philosophical revisionism might take the form of *skepticism* if after revising some type of discourse, we find that what we thought the discourse expressed does not exist. One might then adopt an error theory about the use of the discourse. To give one example from metaethics, John Mackie proposes that when people make moral judgments they take themselves to be referring to some kind of moral property "out there" in the world.[11] Mackie argues that ordinary understanding is committed to the idea that moral properties are genuine properties of the world. After arguing that there are no such properties, he concludes that ordinary understanding is in error. He thus adopts an "error theory" of moral judgment. In contrast, Alasdair Mac-

Intyre's revisionism rests on a cultural analysis of morality.[12] According to MacIntyre, our contemporary moral vocabulary is composed of a variety of pieces of moral tradition that have been taken out of the original context in which they once made sense. When we had, for example, a firm conception of "good for humans in general" we could coherently evaluate virtues, actions, social practices, and the like. Lacking such an account in the modern era, we are left with confused and incoherent moral discourse.

What are we to make of these revisions? Are everyday moral beliefs distorted or incoherent? I think that one might be justly skeptical of any attempt to capture what common sense means in a discourse as complex as "morality." Therefore, revisionist accounts are always open to the challenge of demonstrating the accuracy of their accounts of common sense. Nevertheless, let's hazard a few observations about our current moral sensibilities. We are living at a time in U.S. culture in which interpretations of morality oscillate between extreme subjectivism and extreme absolutism. Interestingly enough, we find philosophical revisionist skeptics in the common culture, people who, with Mackie or MacIntyre, believe that something is radically amiss with the conceptual framework of morality. Can we identify briefly the features of morality that lead philosophers and ordinary people into revisionist skepticism? Here's a try:

(1)   Morality is comprised of fixed rules or principles. These are "fixed" in the sense that if they apply to a given situation, they cannot be overridden. Moral principles comprise a consistent set of rules for the resolution of any moral conflict.

(2)   Moral principles reflect a moral reality that transcends the particulars of human perceptions, judgments, activities, practices, and institutions. Although moral principles guide human conduct, and thus bear on human motivation, their authority rests on sources independent of the particular contingencies of human nature.

I don't pretend that these statements capture everything that everyone means by "morality." I do think that views such as these reflect pervasive interpretations of morality that tend to feed projects of revisionist skepticism. Consider how a pragmatist revision of these might look:

(1?)   Moral principles are not rules to perform specific actions, but considerations that should regulate our judgments about hard cases.

(2?)   Moral norms grow out of human practices and activities. Their *meaning* and their *justificatory authority* reside in their role in helping to realize values internal to human practices. Morality is not a consistent set of beliefs. Rather, moral considerations are heterogeneous, involving elements of indeterminacy and inconsistency. To the extent that we can resolve problems that result from indeterminacy and inconsistency, we must do so by carefully attending to the particular functions or roles of moral considerations.

Note that the pragmatist wants to go on using moral discourse, believing that morality has an indispensible role in human culture, but claims that this role can only be understood properly by treating moral considerations as in many respects importantly like other kinds of nonmoral practical considerations. Morality is like medicine and engineering, in that it is located in learned ways of acting within a community, and it is revisable under new circumstances. This is an alternative strategy to revisionist skepticism. Pragmatism is a revisionist *reconstruction* of morality. The reconstructive strategy seeks to salvage some of the ordinary understanding of morality. It does not abandon moral discourse wholesale. However, to the extent that ordinary understanding rejects the contingent sources of morality in human practices, pragmatism is at odds with common sense. Such revision, if done properly, ought to help us use the discourse to manage practices and activities more intelligently. This pragmatist strategy is not easy to defend. Defenders of the discourse under reconstruction will suspect skeptical assault. Skeptics will suspect a failure of intellectual nerve. Both sides will charge a kind of middle-of-the-road compromising attitude that is apt to lead to hypocrisy or self-deception. Despite all of these dangers, I maintain that pragmatic reconstruction remains the best hope for setting the house of moral philosophy in order. The pragmatist conceptual reconstruction in this book is offered with the hope that ethical theory's conceptual tools will be of use in the critical evaluation of social practices.

Relationship to Other Pragmatist Studies

I consider this book to be a development of pragmatism in the area of moral theory. There is no universal consensus among pragmatists about how to approach morality, nor is there universal consensus on what it takes for a view to be "pragmatist." The case here is similar to feminism—there are many pragmatisms and many feminisms. I do think of my pragmatism as "Deweyan" because the book frequently draws on his ethical writing and his theory of habits. I am aware that the word "pragmatism" has come to represent an array of philosophical positions. I have no special attachment to the word "pragmatism" and would be happy to insert some other label in its place if the many connotations of "pragmatism" get in the way of taking my position at face value. I use the label partly because the position that I defend here did not develop during a solitary meditation. Most of the philosophers (living and dead) to whom I owe a debt of gratitude feel comfortable calling themselves "pragmatists," even though the views they defend might only bear a family resemblance to each other. So, I describe my position with the term "pragmatism," in part, in order to express grateful acknowledgment of how I got to where I am now.

Nevertheless, a book that takes the body of Dewey's concepts and ideas for transplant into metaethics in the current context faces the dangers that come with any delicate operation. We need to make sure that Deweyan ideas nourish their new theoretical body. Moreover, the new body and the old organs will change each other. The only way to judge my success is in the details of the argument itself. All I can ask before the argument is set out is that Dewey scholars and nonpragmatist moral philosophers remain open to this kind of fusion. Those looking for a comprehensive interpretation and defense of Dewey's own theory will not find it in this book. To date, the best book-length account of Dewey's ethical theory, in my view, is Jennifer Welchman's *Dewey's Ethical Thought*.[13] Gregory Pappas' "Dewey's Ethics: Morality as Experience,"[14] also merits attention.

It is worth stressing that mining Dewey's ideas for new purposes is no offense to the philosopher's shade. Quite the contrary! Dewey never viewed theories as fixed, nor did he think that to be a pragmatist involved accepting a set of fixed doctrines expressed in a theoretical language that ought not be changed. To take an example, Dewey worked long and hard on refining a determinate theoretical account of "experience." As important as "experience" is for any complete understanding of Dewey's own philosophy, "experience" is less fecund than his theory of habits for the purposes of contemporary metaethics. My book is developed with an eye to the current situation in moral theory and thus responds in good pragmatic fashion to the current conceptual landscape. Pragmatists view inquiry as a cooperative enterprise. Thus, although their theoretical assumptions will differ from nonpragmatist philosophers now working in the area of moral theory, they should recognize the importance of communicating with those philosophers in order to find areas of common ground.

My project of building on Dewey's theory of habits is inspired by some recent inquiry. In the theory of rationality, the best example is Frederick Will's theory of norms.[15] In moral theory James D. Wallace's work is exemplary of updated pragmatism. Wallace works out the view that moral considerations are a kind of practical knowledge in two books: *Moral Relevance and Moral Conflict*[16] and *Ethical Norms, Particular Cases*.[17] My book develops the metaethical implications of pragmatism's focus on norms or habits in a way that extends some of the central elements of Wallace's view. Finally, an excellent compact presentation of the import of Dewey's theory of habits for moral theory can be found in Hugh LaFollette's "Pragmatic Ethics."[18]

With respect to various "neopragmatisms," this book goes beyond the influential work of Richard Rorty and Hilary Putnam.

Putnam has written a few articles on pragmatism and morality that focus on the way pragmatism challenges the so-called fact/value dichotomy. However, Putnam's arguments do not make use of the notion of habits. My account of social criticism as "local" is similar to Rorty's ethnocentric pragmatism, which emphasizes solidarity in a community over objectivity as a trans-communal realm. However, my account of social criticism is defended by detailed moral argument, which is frequently lacking in Rorty. Rorty is content to rest his defense of pragmatism on denials of realist projects and affirmations of solidarity with like-minded liberals. Like Rorty, my book adopts a "holistic" account of moral knowledge, but it does so within the framework of "habits" and not that of Rorty's preferred "vocabularies." The focus on habits helps to avoid the impression that pragmatism is a kind of "idealism"—a charge frequently leveled against Rorty.

1 | *A Pragmatic Account of Practical Knowledge*

This chapter offers a pragmatist account of how practical knowledge functions in value deliberation and rational conduct. My theory is meant to account for aesthetic, practical, and cognitive values—as well as those values narrowly defined as "moral." The pragmatist denies a radical difference between moral and nonmoral practical considerations, especially with respect to the kinds of practical knowledge found in each. Thus it is crucial to clarify the pragmatist view of practical knowledge before elucidating what pragmatism has to say about ethical knowledge.

The notion that practical reason is concerned with fixed ends crops up in a variety of accounts of moral and nonmoral rationality. Even though many philosophers have abandoned the notion of fixed ends in nature, they have retained the assumption of fixed ends in other forms, more or less unwittingly. In fact, this assumption is so taken for granted that we find surprisingly few arguments pertaining to it. Pragmatism—especially Dewey's variety—sets out to thoroughly purge fixed ends from our philosophical accounts of rationality. Our views of practical reason ought to do justice to the evolutionary standpoint of the world around us. We live in a moving world, and we are continuously learning about this world and our conduct in it. We must be mindful that our models of practical reason do not distort the very practical life that gives birth to them. Models of practical reasoning are like maps. We don't confuse the map with the land that it represents—a land rich in detail, and always in a process of change.

The first section of this chapter sets out the fixed-end account of practical knowledge, including some arguments for the view. The second section begins to develop the pragmatist alternative by exploring the functions of practical knowledge in arts and practices like cooking, hunting, baseball, or house building. Focusing on such practices vividly illustrates the pragmatist view that practical knowledge is located in learned, socially shared habits. The third section uses the pragmatist view of practical knowledge to explain basic structural features of practical justification. Finally, the fourth section shows how the pragmatist view of practical knowledge is further supported by the light it sheds on motivation.

Many accounts of practical reason separate the cognitive and evaluative elements of practical reason. Practical considerations have two components: (1) values and (2) beliefs based on relevant information about how best to achieve those values. The pragmatist view that I defend throws this sort of separation into question. This chapter explores the structure of practical knowledge, and Chapter 2 deals with values. Essentially, I start with the very distinction between practical knowledge and value that is so central to the fixed-end account of rationality. A perspicuous rendering of practical knowledge will motivate a view that cannot sustain the division between the evaluative and the cognitive.

FIXED-END ACCOUNTS OF PRACTICAL KNOWLEDGE:
BASIC ASSUMPTIONS

It may be misleading to refer to the fixed-end account as a "view," since it is not really a complete theory of rational conduct, but rather a pervasive assumption behind a variety of theories. The fixed-end view gets some of its plausibility from some noncontroversial assumptions about rational conduct. Let's explore these assumptions. Rational conduct, as I understand it, includes the class of human actions based on practical knowledge used to pursue practical purposes. These purposes typically represent values or goods. Practical knowledge and some value taken as a goal are the two major constituents of rational conduct. I take this conceptual point to be noncontroversial. At the most basic level, we distinguish rational from nonrational or irrational action on the basis of the idea that rational action is informed by practical considerations used in the pursuit of one or more goals. I am using the term "rational" in a minimal sense, not in the sense of "ideally" rational. "Rational" is a normative predicate. We need a full-blown philosophical theory of rationality to offer an account of what it is to be ideally rational. The minimal sense that I have in mind here is more like "candidate for the ideally rational."[1]

A second noncontroversial assumption: rational conduct may be divided into two classes: bare intentional actions, and actions based on practical reasoning. Many actions that we perform, such as raising an arm, turning off a light, opening a window, and tying a shoe, are intentional but do not typically involve reflective deliberation. The practical knowledge in many of these actions is a kind of "know-how." Such knowledge usually involves skill in appropriate response more than it does explicit propositional belief, let alone beliefs or judgments supported by arguments. The valued goals in these actions are also not typically in the front of consciousness when the actions are performed. However, in most cases, if the action was intentional, a person could give some explanation of the good of what she was trying reach through the action (e.g., answer a question, get ready for bed, cool off a room, prepare to go for a walk).[2]

In practical reasoning, we are often concerned with *justifying* our actions—with finding out what would be best to do. Such practical reasoning involves certain beliefs about what goals are worth pursuing and certain beliefs about information relevant to achieving these goals. I want to be a successful lawyer, so I gather information about law schools in order to arrive at a decision about what schools merit an application. I believe that I am obligated to help the poor, so I explore all of the volunteer activities available to me in order to decide which one to join. I enjoy roller coaster rides, so I make plans to visit an amusement park every summer. The standard concern in practical reasoning is to arrive at judgments about what would be good or bad to do.

Third, rational conduct involves being *motivated* to take certain practical considerations seriously. Practical reasoning is action-guiding, in the sense that we are frequently moved by its conclusions. Intentional actions may not always be based on explicit judgments, but they are motivated by intentions and practical knowledge.

These three assumptions about rational conduct need to be accounted for in any theory of rationality, and this chapter treats each in turn. I take the antipragmatist fixed-end view to be an account of the *structure* of explanation and justification of action. I shall argue that the fixed-end view is seriously flawed.

Before going further, let's define these two views of structure:

> FEI: Intentional actions are explained by practical knowledge that involves two components: a grasp of some end E accepted as a value, and one or more beliefs about how the action contributes to the realization of E. These beliefs may be either implicit or explicit.

> FEJ: Some end E accepted as a value must serve as the justificatory ground for an action. The practical knowledge that figures in justifications of actions consists of one or more beliefs about how the action contributes to the realization of E.

Before offering arguments for the fixed-end view, we need to understand just how entrenched the view is among contemporary theorists. One important recent debate in ethics is between consequentialists and defenders of agent-relative morality. Some consequentialists hold that the only moral requirement is to do whatever will bring about the best results. This consequentalist reason is agent-neutral, in the sense that it says that anyone should always choose to do whatever among the available alternatives will maximize good. Defenders of agent-relative morality attack this idea. They hold, roughly, that we are sometimes bound by reasons that are relative to a person. A mother might, for example, have a reason to favor her own child in a rescue situation because this child is hers, even if doing so does not bring about more overall good (e.g., it is possible to let the child die and save the doctor with a cure for cancer). Agent-relative moralities maintain that some reasons make such essential reference to a person. In this case such essential reference shows up in the reason "My child ought to be saved before others."[3]

Notice that despite their differences, consequentialists and agent-relative theorists both hold the notion that there must be some end or some reason that functions as a justifier relative to an instance of practical reasoning. The debate here is about what kinds of reasons we have. The parties to the debate do not doubt the adequacy of the basic idea that practical justification must be grounded in reasons that express practical ends taken as values. Both consequentialists and their critics accept a certain picture of the justificatory structure but differ about what items fit into that structure and how to extend the basic structure into a fuller theoretical account.

In what follows, I argue that the fixed-end view of justificatory structure distorts important features of practical reason, which are better illuminated through the pragmatist theory of habits. The fixed-end view is such a basic, taken-for-granted assumption that it is difficult to find much in the way of argument for it. In the next two sections, I do my best to cull these arguments from various philosophical texts.

ARGUMENTS FOR FIXED-END ACCOUNTS OF INTENTIONAL ACTION AND JUSTIFICATION

The first argument for the fixed-end view of intentional action is that such ends are required to answer a "why" question that can be raised about any candidate for intentional action. In her *Intention,* G. E. M. Anscombe argues that when we explain a person's intentional action, we must make reference to some claim about what the person regards as good—as making the action worth doing. To the question, "Why is he planting the garden?"

we might answer "Because he wants fresh vegetables." But at some point, we must end our search for action explanations by citing something that the man regards as good. For example, we might simply conclude that he regards the pleasure of freshly grown vegetables as good. Or he might take his wife's pleasure in consuming the vegetables as a good.

Nothing yet follows about the nature of this good or the standards for determining what is good. What seems to follow from these observations is that the assumption that an act is intentional presupposes that we can ask and answer a "why" question about what the person is trying to do. Eventually, our answer must be given in terms of some account of what the person regards as a good. Our explanation could be given either by a third-party observer or the person himself.[4] The fact that such an explanation could be furnished does not, however, imply that it has to figure in the mind of the person herself at the time of action.

We need to keep distinct the question of why someone performed an action from the question of whether that action was justified. I can show that the act of speeding down the freeway at one hundred miles per hour is intentional because the driver had a pro-attitude of "wanting to get to the next rest stop as soon as possible to use the toilet" and the belief that "speeding at one hundred miles per hour is the best way to satisfy that want" without thereby being committed to the idea that he had a *good reason* for breaking the speed limit.

It is commonly held that justification of an action involves showing the reason for it. This thought is connected quite naturally to the idea that a person has a reason for some action *A* if it can be shown that doing *A* advances some end that she accepts as a value. So, a person might believe that she has a reason for the action of driving her car past the speed limit because she has the valued end of "quickly relieving herself at the toilet." The practical knowledge that figures in such justifications is knowledge of means, including knowledge of actions, that seem required to achieve the end. What justifies the action—what gives it a reason—is the end itself.

This view of justification can be defended by a regress argument. Regress arguments are common in foundationalist theories of knowledge, and a brief comparison with these may prove helpful. A basic structural feature of such theories is that in order for a person to have knowledge, her reasons for belief must be based on some foundational belief that is not itself questionable. For any belief *P,* we can ask for a reason why we are justified in asserting that we know that *P* is true. For any reason *R,* we can continue to ask for a further reason why we are justified in asserting that we know that *R* is true. It would seem that we are faced either with an infinite regress of reasons for reasons or with a circular argument if we block the regress by some member of the justificatory chain. One way out of the alleged regress is to find some foundational beliefs that cannot be questioned— that do not require further reasons for their warrant. These beliefs are in some way self-certifying. To have them is to know that they must be true. Now, foundationalists may debate the nature of the self-certifying beliefs. Rationalists hold that the foundations are clear and distinct innate ideas. Empiricists claim that the foundations are based on beliefs about perceptual episodes. Nonetheless, both schools agree about the structure of the theory. The disagreement is about the content of the theory.

Compare these observations about foundationalist epistemology to a similar kind of foundationalism in the fixed-end view of practical justification. Fixed-end theorists may disagree about whether the ends that figure in reasons for action are weighted desires, non-desire-based reasons, or some overarching goal like happiness. But they agree that some such end must play the justificatory role. After all, for any reason *R* given in support of some action *A,* one can ask why *R* is a good thing. At some point we must terminate the justificatory chain in some end taken as a good in itself.

Hume and Aristotle make the regress argument. They make it in the context of viewing ends in terms of "passions" and "desires." But they could apply the argument to any theory of practical reason—even one that does not believe that all practical justification must terminate in some end that appeals to a desire or passion. Aristotle writes, "We do not choose everything because of something else, since if we do, it will go on without limit, making desire empty and futile."[5] Aristotle concludes there must be some basic good desired for itself.

Hume makes a related argument. He writes,

> The ultimate ends of human actions can never, in any case be accounted for by reason, but recommend themselves entirely to the sentiments and affections of mankind, without any dependence on the intellectual faculties. Ask a man, why he uses exercise; he will answer, because he desires to keep his health. If you enquire, why he desires health, he will readily reply, because sickness is painful. If you push enquiries farther, and desire a reason, why he hates pain, it is impossible he can ever given any. This is an ultimate end, and he is never referred to any other object. . . . It is impossible there can be a progress in infinitum; and that one thing can always be a reason, why another is desired. Something must be desirable on its own account, and because of its immediate accord or agreement with human sentiment and affection.[6]

Hume accepts the fixed-end view of the structure of practical justification. He fills that view in with the claim that these ends must agree with human sentiments or passions because he believes that without such sentiments reason alone cannot influence conduct.

The regress argument could be offered to account for the structure of either the explanation of intentional action or the justification of action. When I explain your action of jogging three miles every morning, the argument goes, I must make reference to some end or ends that you believe makes your action of jogging worth doing: a more appealing physical appearance or a healthier circulatory system. When you explain why your action of jogging three miles every morning is a good thing to do, it appears that you must make reference to some basic ends taken as good. It may turn out that the ends you refer to in a justification are the same ends that explain why your act is intentional. Although it is true that many times explanation and justification converge, they can obviously diverge as well. Not every intentional act is justified or rational.[7]

Practical Knowledge: A Habit-Based Account

In what follows I argue that the fixed-end view of justificatory structure distorts practical knowledge as it is used in ordinary instances of intentional action and in the justification of action. The idea that practical justification is grounded in fixed ends is flawed, in part, because it fails to illuminate a range of problem-solving cases. That is, the fixed end fails to make sense of *learning processes* that occur when we seek justifications for changes in practice. This flaw is embedded in the minimum conception of justificatory *structure*—a flaw that exists regardless of how we might fill out the minimum conception with worked-out theories of ideal rationality or value theories.

KNOW-HOW, NOVELTY, COMPLEXITY

I begin with some commonplace observations about skilled expertise in practices. Any developed practice such as cooking or playing a musical instrument can only be successfully pursued by people who have internalized practical norms. Cooking a gourmet meal well requires years of training. Those educated in norms of cooking are able to interact skillfully with a practical context consisting of implements, tools, materials, and the like. An expert cook sees ingredients *as* potential constituents of certain dishes. She sees tools as implements for certain tasks. The novice, when confronted with the same kitchen as the expert chef, does not see the situation in the same way because he lacks the relevant skills and knowledge required to prepare the meal. This brings me to the first important fact of practical life: skilled expertise involves a *know-how* that is not best represented as action resulting from judgments about rules. When one has acquired expertise, one transcends the use of rules and simply does what the situation calls for.[8]

The second fact of practical life is that activities change over time as a result of the solution of *novel problems*. In a quite straight-forward sense, the activity of cooking precedes the particular projects of an individual cook. Cooking is a tradition with a his-tory. Over time, new ways of doing things are discovered and old ways modified or rejected. This continual modification of the activity is the result of the trials and experimentation of particu-lar cooks. But it is also the result of other changes that indirectly modify the practice of cooking (e.g., electric ovens; food proces-sors; imported spices, fruits, and vegetables; etc.). The expert cook is able to frame problems and devise solutions in ways that go beyond existing practical knowledge. The problem solving of an expert cook advances and modifies the activity. That is, the ex-pert is able to modify the activity in significant ways unavailable to a novice (except, perhaps, by accident). These advances may be written down in a set of practical propositions, perhaps in a new cookbook. However, this general knowledge is always sub-ject to modification, revision, or reinterpretation in light of par-ticular circumstances.

The sheer *complexity* of practical life is a third fact that fol-lows close on the heels of the fact of novelty. The expert cook does not mechanically follow directions laid down in a textbook of cooking. She is able to modify, change, and further her prac-tice through skilled execution. The pursuit of a complex enter-prise such as cooking can never be encapsulated in a set of rules or directions. The considerations that go into practicing this art well are highly circumstantial: for example, What ingredient may be substituted for this dish? What sorts of people frequent this restaurant? What sorts of economic resources are available to purchase new equipment? The permutation of circumstances rel-evant to a cook's particular judgments does not imply that her responses are arbitrary. Rather, it implies that the sort of skilled judgment or sense of propriety she must exercise can never be encapsulated in a code of propositions or rules.

So far I have focused on expertise, offering what we might think of as a brief phenomenology of salient facts about such expertise. Let's briefly to turn to the novice. Notice that with re-spect to our three facts, know-how, novelty, and complexity, the novice's actions are less fluid than the expert's. The novice needs to engage in more reflective deliberation about her actions because she does not have the skill to see things in ways that trigger immediate, appropriate response. She is not able to solve novel problems in such a way as to significantly modify the activity. The activity itself is novel *to her*. With respect to complexity, the basic skills, tasks, tools, and instruments that the expert can take for granted are experienced by the beginner as a bewildering array of foreign material.

From these facts about practical life we can infer a plausible conclusion about practical rules. Beliefs about such rules are *usually* indispensable for the *beginner*. The novice uses such rules as guides for learning about what is important in some activity, especially through a process of decomposing a practical endeavor into its component parts. Although it seems likely that assimilating rules is often a necessary condition for development of skill in some activity, we can think of cases in which such assimilation is not required. Language use is a good case. One learns rules of grammar long after gaining a solid grasp of the language. In short, practical rules, for the novice, are usually necessary but far from sufficient for the successful assimilation of a skill or practice.

Similar points can be made about the expert. From time to time the expert will need to fall back on beliefs about rules when she faces novel situations or problems. These practical rules are modified as novel problems are solved. However, intellectual grasp and application of practical rules are far from sufficient for displaying skilled expertise. The complexity of circumstances, the need for skilled know-how, and the novelty of problems all support the hypothesis that practical rules are at best useful intellectual tools for efficient organization of practical life when we need to learn new things. Whether one is a novice or an expert, rules function to help us learn about our circumstances so that we may solve problems and reach new levels of mastery, efficiency, and control. Practical judgments and responses can never be completely encoded in a set of rules or principles.

The fixed-end view of intentional action holds that practical knowledge is knowledge of how best to accomplish some end a person regards as good. The explanation of action turns on identifying an end held as good and on certain key beliefs about how best to realize that end. The conclusion that I have reached thus far is that the beliefs about what is appropriate to do—beliefs about the relevant practical rules—play a limited role in structured practices. Do similar points apply to intentional actions outside structured practices? Take simple intentional actions such as flipping light switches, waving hello, turning on a faucet, opening a window, or flipping a yo-yo. It seems odd to say that these actions involve complex circumstances on the grounds that they cannot be codified in practical rules or that they sometimes require creative improvisation. Why wouldn't the fixed-end account be appropriate to explain these simple intentional actions?

Simple actions seem different from actions within structured practices because we tend to take for granted the complex background required to make sense of even very simple bits of behavior. Turning off a light switch may be further described in any number of ways, depending on the context.[9] It may be "the first step in preparation for love-making," "closing the act of a play," "getting ready for bed," "saving electricity," and so forth. The best description in a given case may simply be, "This is the action a person does when entering and exiting rooms in her house." But even so, such a description will be part of a larger network of assumptions about what she tends to do in her house.

Typically, we do not focus on the complex background of such simple acts. We engage in such analysis of simple acts when we have some concern or special purpose—usually when something has gone wrong. We may be interested in why the light switch was flipped when, for example, a stagehand misses a cue during a performance of a play. We may then set out to learn who flipped the switch and what that person took herself to be trying to do. When we do engage in such an analysis, we become aware of a complex background of assumptions needed to comprehend the meaning of a particular intentional act. This background is also needed to determine whether a particular act is intentional.

When I deny that intentional action is best explained in terms of beliefs about practical rules paired with accepted ends, I do not mean to deny that beliefs and accepted ends are in no way involved in intentional actions. The point is that belief-end pairs do not adequately explain what it is to have practical knowledge. The practical knowledge that figures in both first- and third-person explanations of intentional actions is better accounted for in terms of interpenetrating, shared habits. I turn now to the more adequate view of practical knowledge. A few preliminary words are in order.

The account of habits that I offer is *holist* in the sense that I maintain that one cannot understand the meaning and function of habits independently of understanding their interrelations with each other and with the complex circumstances in which they function. The holistic functioning of habits has diachronic and synchronic dimensions. In what follows, I distinguish three dimensions of habits. The first, *interpenetration,* displays both diachronic and synchronic properties. The second, *functional interaction,* is synchronic. The third, *historical transmission,* is diachronic. I do not regard these three dimensions of habits as ontologically separable. However, for purposes of analysis, it is helpful to divide habits in these ways. I begin with interpenetration because it strikes me as the easiest way to begin an exposition of the pragmatist account of habits.

COMPOSITION/INTERPENETRATION OF HABITS

The fixed-end account of practical knowledge distorts our understanding of rational conduct in even the most routine, pre-reflective displays of skill. The fixed-end view misses the ways in which skilled action depends upon interpenetrating habits. The rational guidance of an action does not occur by matching action to single rule but rather by the mutual interaction of many habits.

Frederick Will refers to the phenomenon of interpenetrating habits as the "composition" of norms.[10] Consider a particular action such as cooking a meal at a restaurant. This action is carried out not by the serial application of one rule followed by another. It is not as if the cook first sees the fillet smoking and then applies the rule, "When fillets smoke and turn translucent, you ought to turn them over." The person confronted with a cooking task simultaneously mobilizes a host of habits, including physical abilities, perceptual abilities, a cultural familiarity with aesthetic norms of food preparation, and so forth. Using the term "practice," Will writes,

> One who learns a practice as if he were a solider being imprinted with elements of close-order drill learns to behave in a way so odd and eccentric that Bergson could make it an important element in his theory of laughter. One essential thing missing from such learning is an understanding of how the more obvious, immediate responses that exemplify practices are determined in character by features of the conditions of performance, including therewith other dispositions to act, other forms of procedure, in short, other practices. This means that in following practices one is performing in a way that is governed in a great degree and in a highly complex way. . . . Practices do, so to speak, confront circumstances, but not as individuals. Rather, in the metaphor employed by W. V. Quine in speaking of the coordination of statements with sense experience, they do so as corporate bodies.[11]

Part of Will's point is that even the most spontaneous skilled responses presuppose a complex structure that he calls "conditions of performance." The conditions include the interacting habits and the concrete features of the context of action. Particular responses arise out of a larger context of background habits or norms. Philosophers of science have adopted a similar holism in understanding how scientific statements and hypotheses are properly tested. The idea, roughly, is that we cannot look at the acceptability of a hypothesis simply in terms of whatever tests would falsify the statement. A hypothesis might not be confirmed by an experimental test but could still be acceptable in light of sufficient revisions of other auxiliary assumptions associated with the theory in question. Similarly, one might say that the appropriateness of a practical response can be adequately determined only through the application of a host of practical considerations and not just any single one.

Dewey develops an interesting account of habits in *Human Nature and Conduct* that emphasizes the holistic, interpenetrating property of practical considerations. Not to be thought of as mechanical rote responses, habits for Dewey are dynamic response patterns that help to focus behavior and attention. We should think of habits broadly as concrete ways of thinking, feeling, and doing. A habit can show up in many practices and activities. Its character and meaning can be determined only in light of its role in an activity or practice and its connections to other habits. The fact that habits can only be interpreted in light of such a holistic context makes it difficult initially to characterize their meaning in abstraction from their function in particular contexts. Consider the range of qualities that might be called Deweyan habits:

- impatience as a personality trait (showing up in a certain style of dealing with problems);
- a tendency to hard drinking after hours;
- skill in manipulating sensitive implements and tools;
- an excellent singing voice;
- class prejudice (manifested in treatment of menial laborers on the job);
- skill in improvising dishes;
- loyalty to all things Roman Catholic;
- commitment to moral principles of truth-telling and fair play;
- speaking English and French fluently.

To make such a list of habits runs the risk of misrepresenting their character, since habits should not be identified with their symbolic expressions (either in the agent herself or in the analyst studying behavior). Dewey's use of the term "habit" is initially difficult to grasp because of a tendency to think of a habit as a specific, fixed pattern of action. We forget that habits change over time, partly because of the influence of other habits, partly because of changing circumstances. We also forget that what a habit means depends on our purposes and problems in specific contexts.

Interpenetration is both a synchronic and a diachronic property of habits. Interpenetration refers to the fact that a habit always functions with other habits in a holistic context. A singing habit, for instance, may *synchronically* express itself with other habits such as participation in religious services, interactions with a choir, and so forth. These habits develop over time, *diachronically*, from childhood. Notice further that habits interpenetrate within a person and between many people.

HABITS AND TRANSACTIONS

A person's habits are in transaction or functional interaction with multilayered environments. Transaction with environments is a synchronic feature of habits. Acquired habits are functions similar to breathing or seeing. At any given moment, habits are in some kind of functional transaction with an environment in the here and now. As Dewey puts it, "Habits may profitably be compared to physiological functions, like breathing, digesting. The latter are, to be sure, involuntary, while habits are acquired. But important as this difference is for many purposes it should not conceal the fact that habits are functions in many respects, and especially in requiring the cooperation of organism and environment."[12] The physiological function of breathing requires both lung and air. But air and lung are not "externally" connected; rather, they are functions that mutually modify each other. Socially learned habits like house building depend on both physical and cultural environments. The kinds of houses we build depend on the available materials, the type of physical environment, the level of technology of a culture and so on.[13]

The continual transaction of habits with an environment makes sense of a certain indeterminacy vis-à-vis habits and circumstances. Even in the most routine application of rules to cases we cannot know from cursory inspection what actions are appropriate. We must take into consideration Will's "conditions of performance." These include "both personal aspects of those engaged in the performances and aspects of the impersonal environment in which they are performing. In this terminology, the personal environment of any particular performance will include, as a most important component, many and varied other dispositions to act with which any given disposition is related and which may inhibit, intensify, or otherwise modify its realization."[14]

HABITS AS HISTORICAL TRANSMISSIONS

Historical transmission is a diachronic property of habits. A habit has a particular history in the life of a particular person as well as in the lives of generations of people.[15] The practices of the Roman Catholic church and the vocation of a priest are historically transmitted habits. A person acquires a habit, usually early in youth, and then develops the habit throughout childhood. Unfortunately, many habits, like pitching baseball, are prone to degeneration well before our lives are spent. Although habits are historically transmitted in the lives of individuals, they reside in evolving practices and institutions like churches, technologies, arts, and sciences. Thus, we can view the Roman Catholic Church as a set of historically transmitted habits.

Acknowledging historical transmission in institutions and practices helps to focus awareness on the fact that what we do now with our habits will shape those who come after us. Dewey writes, "Individuals flourish and wither away like the grass of the fields. But the fruits of their work endure and make possible the development of further activities having fuller significance. It is of grace not of ourselves that we lead civilized lives. There is sound sense in the old pagan notion that gratitude is the root of all virtue." Acknowledging our dependence supports a moral obligation to take care of our current habits and their environments for the sake of those who will come later. That is, the only way to repay the debt of gratitude to those who came before is to ensure that worthy projects they began continue to flourish or improve. Dewey says, "Loyalty to whatever in the established environment makes a life of excellence possible is the beginning of all progress. The best we can accomplish for posterity is to transmit unimpaired and with some increment of meaning the environment inherited from our forerunners, and it is enhanced as we foresee the fruits of our labors in the world in which our successors live."[17] Certainly the fact that habits are historically transmitted does not imply that we are passive recipients of the transmission process. As we apply these transmits to our circumstances, we are capable of shaping their character to some degree. One only need explore the history of an art such as jazz improvisation in order to appreciate the ways in which traditions are modified during the course of their use.[18]

I mention the fact that habits are socially shared historical transmissions because it is important not to be mislead by terminology. Metaphysically speaking, a habit is not simply a property of physical or bodily behavior (although these are elements of habits). In many cases, habits embody deep-seated commitments of the self, especially identification of the self with the ideals and aspirations of some particular community. Although it might seem strained to refer to such sociopsychological attitudes as the Israeli attachment to Jerusalem as habits, these attitudes represent approved ways of regarding land handed down from history. Such habits are no doubt highly complex and sophisticated, presupposing many complicated social customs that embed patterns of evaluation and belief. Nonetheless, we can view these as habits in Dewey's sense of complex social functions. The pragmatist approach maintains that morality is more analogous to nonmoral practical skills and arts like medicine, cookery, and baseball than has been acknowledged by most of the tradition of moral philosophy. This analogy should not obscure the sense in which habits have a history that contributes to the *deep self-understanding* of those who have acquired them.[19]

Let's take stock of the argument so far. The fixed-end account of practical knowledge is impoverished failing to account for the limits of beliefs about practical rules in light of three facts: know-how, novelty, and complexity. Secondly, I have argued that the fixed-end account distorts the nature of even very routine action guided by practical knowledge. Practical knowledge involves having habits with a three-fold dimension that includes:

(1) transactions with particular circumstances occasioning practical judgments and responses;

(2) the interpenetration of habits; and

(3) the historical transmission of habits.

These three dimensions of habits militate against any account of practical knowledge that reduces the latter to beliefs about rules paired with accepted ends. The practical knowledge that figures in intentional action is constituted by habits with the three aforementioned dimensions. Practical knowledge figures in reflective judgments and in relatively unreflective skilled responses (as when an expert does only what the situation requires). Practical judgments and responses presupposes habits of thinking, feeling, and doing that are internal to a person's psychological economy and that are shared with others. These habits are social in another sense: they are located in historically transmitted activities and practices that transcend particular individuals. As individuals use habits to respond to problems, these responses sometimes change the character of those habits.

Practical Reason and Continuous Learning

The fixed-end theorist might concede that a richly developed holistic understanding of the context of habits is needed to explain the function of practical knowledge adequately. However, such a theorist might say that something like the fixed-end view must still apply to the structure of practical justification. When we make decisions about what we have good reason to do, what changes in conduct might be warranted, and so forth, we must justify our practical decisions in terms set by the structure of the fixed-end account. Recall that structure:

FEJ: Some end *E* accepted as a value must serve as the justificatory ground for an action. The practical knowledge that figures in justifications of actions is one or more beliefs about how the action contributes to the realization of *E*.

FEJ could be filled in with any number of accounts of *E*. *E* might be a state such as "pleasure." *E* might be a reason for action, specified functionally in terms of whatever provides grounds for an action. *E* might be a set of desires that a person has or a set of principles. A fixed-end theorist might also point out that no commitment need be made to the notion that the justificatory end is *so* fixed that it cannot be revised in light of future deliberation. The claim that *E* is "fixed" minimally means that *E* is fixed relative to a stretch of deliberative justification. So a sophisticated defender of a minimalist fixed-end account of justificatory structure might well join Dewey in rejecting the view that there are final ends beyond action—ends that may be eternal or a priori in some Platonic sense. If "fixed ends" means simply those ends that justify my action here and now, then it is unclear what is gained by rejecting what seems so commonsensical.

I identify two basic failures in even a minimalist fixed-end account of justificatory structure. The first is a distortion of the role of practical justification in *learning*. That is, fixed-end accounts of justification do not correctly account for cases in which educative experience results in the intelligent modification of practices and activities. The second problem is an inadequate account of the process of continual reevaluation of ends over the history of a person or a community.

I must stress again that FEJ is not a complete theory of justification. The ends it speaks of are given a complete (ideal) justification by ethical or value theories. Some theorists hold that the process by which a person arrives at a decision is completely different from the process by which a decision is (ideally) justified. This is especially true for those moral theories that hold that oftentimes the best thing for a deliberator to do is not focus on principles or procedures of justification advocated by the theory.[20] Nonetheless, even views that make a radical split between deliberation and justification still hold that "the thing" that gets the ideal justification is some end fixed relative to a piece of deliberation. Even if the mind that represents the justification of an end is different from the mind that deliberates, we still assume that the objective justification of the *action* flows from a fixed-end to the action. It is this view of justificatory structure that I am putting into question in what follows.

VALUE DELIBERATION: A CASE AND A MODEL

The pragmatist view of practical reason that I defend takes action plans to be the "formal" aim of practical deliberation. Action plans mediate habits. To say that action plans mediate habits is to say that they are "answers" to situations that are problematic in part because old habits fail to work in new circumstances. The generic or formal function of action plans is to mediate habits in the sense that they take us from unsettled to settled situations. In a sense, action plans are attempts to recontextualize conduct by framing a situation in terms of new possibilities.

I will illustrate the pragmatist view through an examination of Jane Addams' account of the crisis that led her to decide to devote her life to a settlement house. Addams' own description is a rich personal narrative. As a pragmatist, Addams' interpretation of her own practical deliberation well illustrates the pragmatist view of practical justification. After examining the case, I offer a generic model of practical justification.

Addams' book *Twenty Years at Hull House* describes a complex fabric of personal and social history. The book chronicles key moments in Addams' own life, as well as the life of Hull House. Hull House was a settlement house designed to minister to the needs of struggling immigrant communities of Chicago in the late nineteenth and early twentieth centuries. Addams describes her "conversion" to participation in a settlement house in an early chapter of *Twenty Years at Hull House*, entitled "The Snare of Preparation." After Addams finished her college education at Rockford Female Seminary, she took two trips to Europe. It was near the end of the last trip to Europe that she decided to abandon plans to become a physician and take up the project of a settlement house. Disgust with a bullfight in Spain led her to a breakthrough in self-understanding. It is clear from the events leading up to this incident that Addams struggled with her own sense of guilt at living a privileged middle-class life dedicated to pursuit of personal and professional development. This guilt was grounded in an acute sympathy for the poor and their struggles. Addams describes a number of key experiences that prompted her to reflect on both her own privileged status and the privileged status of the leisure class in general. She continually calls attention to the ways in which the pursuit and enjoyment of "culture"—arts, literature, science—numb the leisure class to the plight of the poor in industrialized nations. She came to this awareness during her first European trip. She was taken to an auction of decaying fruit and vegetables late on a Saturday night and was overwhelmed by the desperation of the poor. She could not forget their outstretched hands groping for decaying food, writing that her "final impression was not of ragged, tawdry clothing nor of pinched and sallow faces, but of myriads of hands, empty, pathetic, nerveless, and workworn, showing white in the uncertain light of the street, and clutching forward for food which was already unfit to eat."[21] She writes that every subsequent encounter with outstretched hands, be it in a class of children responding to a question, or a calisthenic exercise, reminds her of these hands. The experience was burned into her memory.

Addams has these experiences because she has previously acquired moral habits of sympathy and care. Nevertheless, these experiences awaken new insights into the tension between "care" and "culture." Addams describes this tension by recounting a memory of a first-generation educated girl who thinks of her uneducated working-class mother with some envy of her mother's "happy industry and extenuating obstacles, with undisturbed opportunity to believe that her talents were unusual." With a commentary that could apply to herself, Addams says that this educated girl "has nothing to do with the bitter poverty and the social maladjustment which is all about her, and which, after all, cannot be concealed, for it breaks through poetry and literature in a burning tide which overwhelms her; it peers at her in the form of heavy-laden market women and underpaid street laborers, gibing her with a sense of her uselessness."[22] Shortly before this passage, Addams' indicts herself and her peers directly for "numbing our minds with literature that only served to cloud the really vital situation spread before our eyes."[23] Addams comes to see that the educated classes use cultural pursuits to numb themselves to the pain and suffering of the poor. The leisure class probably does not consciously use the pursuit of culture to numb. However, a certain numbness to painful social reality is a consequence of the personal quest for culture. After her experiences in East London, Addams is so stricken by the poverty that "all huge London came to seem unreal save the poverty in its East End."[24]

It would be inaccurate to say that Addams came to believe that cultural pursuits were a vain waste of time. Her view was rather that "the paralyzing sense of futility of all artistic and intellectual effort [occur] when [it is] disconnected from the ultimate test of the conduct it inspired." She seeks to find a way to connect cultural pursuits with some type of socially useful conduct. Years later Hull House would take "cultural development" seriously enough. The house engaged in a variety of educational projects that included lectures by professors from the University of Chicago. However, far from being an individualistic pursuit of personal enrichment, in Hull House the ideal of cultural development was part and parcel of the project of building community out of disparate ethnic groups whose lives were enriched by shared cultural pursuits.

Addams is clear that creating a settlement house was an action plan that answered the problem she experienced in her own life. After witnessing a bullfight in Spain, she writes,

> I felt myself tried and condemned, not only by this disgusting experience but by the entire moral situation which it revealed. It was suddenly made quite clear to me that I was lulling my conscience by a dreamer's scheme, that a mere paper reform had become a

defense for continued idleness, and that I was making it a raison d'être for going on indefinitely with study and travel. It is easy to become the dupe of a deferred purpose of the promise the future can never keep.[25]

Addams resolved to start a settlement house as soon as she returned to America.

How would the fixed-end view of practical justification describe this case? No doubt it would say that Addams' practical justification of the settlement house plan was grounded in her acceptance of a new "end." This new end might be described as social service to the destitute and poor. Perhaps we could say that Addams also came to subscribe to a second end: providing cultural enrichment to the poor. What Addams learned, according to the fixed-end view, is that her old values were no longer viable. The new ends taken as values served as justificatory reasons for the action of starting a settlement house.

The fixed-end view could reconstruct Addams' practical justification of the plan to found Hull House as a straightforward piece of reasoning from general ends that could be expressed in the form of reasons for action. According to FEJ we model our case as follows:

(1)   If one accepts social service as a value, then one should undertake to use one's time and energy to help others.
(2)   Addams accepts social service as a value.
(3)   Founding Hull House is an appropriate way for Addams to use her time and energy to help others.
(4)   Addams should found Hull House.[26]

The fixed-end view is seductively simple in its modeling of practical justification. What could be more obvious than that when we make a judgment about what would be good to do, we support that judgment with general reasons for action? These reasons are the grounds for or against particular judgments about actions. When we explain (to ourselves or to others) why it is good to do something, we appeal to such general reasons. These reasons represent those practical ends that we accept as values. The practical ends authorize our actions.

The pragmatist need not deny that we can speak of our problems in the way suggested by the simplified argument. However, we must be careful not to mask the complexities that give rise to this simplified argument, including the many ways that a person may have reached similar conclusions. According to the pragmatist, Addams comes to better understand her habits up to, and through, her undergraduate education. Direct experience of the poor prompts her to recontextualize her conduct. She comes to see herself as living in a kind of self-deluded "secondary" reality of privilege. We can schematize the process of practical deliberation resulting in the her plan to start a settlement house as follows:

(1)　There is an indeterminate situation, including a felt sense of trouble due to a failure of habits.

(2)　There is a preliminary interpretation of the problem, including a view of what important goods and evils are at issue.

(3)　Action plans are created that attempt to take account of the important goods and evils at issue.

(4)　These action plans are tested in imaginative trials.

(5)　The most promising plan is tested in actions bringing about change in the situation.

(6)　These steps can be repeated by others or used to explain to others what was learned.[27]

This is a model of what I call a "deliberative event." The schema is an abstract representation of what, for purposes of analysis, are salient features of all deliberative events. We should distinguish between an abstract schema of a deliberative event, a particular representation of a deliberative event, and the deliberative event itself.[28] The deliberative event is a relation between a person, a representation, and a problematic situation. The representation is a sign, in the sense of an interpretive object, for a person about a situation that is problematic in some way. Addams' deliberative event occurs over a period of at least two years, culminating with the decision to start a settlement house.

It is fruitful to think of the representation of a deliberative event as connected to *interpretation*. This means, minimally, that *part* of the aim of practical justification is to clarify the meaning of an indeterminate situation. The other thing "interpretation" helps to bring out is the sense in which the ability to represent deliberative events is itself an acquired habit. It is in effect a second-order habit that is brought to bear on other habits.[29] The ability to generate deliberative events is a habit that people acquire intentionally to redirect or reintegrate habits that fail to work properly. Deliberative events mediate habits. If they work, they serve as intermediaries between broken habits.

The most important element of a deliberative event is the action plan. The action plan is that element of the deliberative event which determines whether or not the deliberative event is "completed." To say that a deliberative event is "completed" is simply to say that the indeterminate situation that gave rise to it has been "determined" through the implementation of an action plan. A particular deliberative event X may be completed but yet engender another indeterminate situation that may require another deliberative event Y.

Until the plan is implemented, the deliberative event is not complete. One class of such incomplete deliberative events includes those that are in some way inadequate for dealing with indeterminate situations. A second class includes those for which an action plan has yet to be carried out. A third class includes those whose action plans are still being formulated in imagination.

Failed deliberative events can yield extremely valuable information. Failures may be due to factors beyond an individual's control, or they may reveal flaws intrinsic to the action plan or in other parts of the representation of the deliberative event. For example, the description of the problem may be inadequate. The action plan may well be an appropriate response to a problem that is not at issue. The action plan may not adequately resolve the indeterminate situation. Perhaps the plan is too vague—expressing a vacuous, yet lofty-sounding ideal. Or the action plan may not be realistic in the current circumstances—perhaps it demands too much of current resources. One might argue that Addams' Hull House experiment is a good example of an action plan that, although inspired with idealism, is not so utopian as to be an unworkable endeavor.

Let's apply the model to Addams' decision to found a settlement house. Addams' indeterminate situation spanned a period of several years. It is not as if her growing guilt about her own idleness brought her life projects to a grinding halt. Rather, she found herself gripped with guilt when, almost against her will, she carefully attended to the poor around her. She came to interpret the problem gradually, over a period of two years. She writes,

> For two years in the midst of my distress over the poverty which, thus suddenly driven into my consciousness, had become the Weltschmerz, there was mingled a sense of futility, of misdirected energy, the belief that the pursuit of cultivation would not in the end bring either solace or relief. I gradually reached the conviction that the first generation of college women had taken their learning too quickly, had departed too suddenly from the active, emotional life led by their grandmothers and great-grandmothers; that the contemporary education of the young women had developed too exclusively the power of acquiring knowledge and of merely receiving impressions; that somewhere in the process of "being educated" they had lost that simple and almost automatic response to the human appeal, that old healthful reaction resulting in activity from the mere presence of suffering or of helplessness; that they are so sheltered and pampered they have no chance even to make the "great refusal."[30]

Addams' interpretation of the problem is quite complex. She relates her own personal habits of self-cultivation to a larger social trend of first-generation college-educated women. These women, so enthralled with the pursuit of "culture," have quickly lost touch with other habits of spontaneous care and sympathy for the downtrodden. These other habits were traditionally associated with women (i.e., the "grandmothers" and "great-grandmothers"). Addams came to formulate the settlement house action plan in her imagination gradually. It is important to see that this plan is an effort to do justice to a variety of qualities that Addams has recognized are not satisfactorily realized in her life or in the lives of many other women of her generation. Her solution to this problem combines elements of care for the needy, shared cultural activities, and the application of educational training to social problems. How settlement houses care for the needy should be fairly obvious. As I mentioned earlier, the second element—shared cultural activities—was a major component of Hull House life in that the house sponsored a myriad of historical, artistic, and scientific cultural activities, including lectures and exhibits. Finally, Addams is quite explicit that settlement houses were laboratories for investigating social problems of the working-class life of urban immigrants. The charter of Hull House makes this clear: Its stated mission was "to provide for a higher civic and social life; to institute and maintain educational and philanthropic enterprises; and to *investigate and improve the conditions in the industrial districts of Chicago.*"[31]

For the pragmatist, Addams' action plan is an attempt to recontextualize habits that no longer yield satisfactory experiences within the current environment. The Hull House plan recontextualizes habits by giving them new meanings under new circumstances. Addams does not simply abandon cultural pursuits in order to return to the spontaneous service of the grandmothers and great-grandmothers. Nor does she live a divided life, spending weekends serving others and pursuing personal advancement the rest of the time. She formulates an action plan that combines habits in a novel way that changes both herself and her social environment. If we think of habits as the ingredients of character, and we think of habits as always in transaction with their environments, then Addams' action plan is an experiment in changing parts of her character and parts of her world.

Addams' deliberative event is completed with the founding of Hull House. At some point after Hull House is up and running Addams may be able to say that the action plan worked to restore harmony to indeterminate circumstances. Nevertheless, Hull House life generates new situations and new habits. These will engender new problems and new occasions for deliberative events. While we live, there is no final end in the sense of a goal that once reached, will terminate activity. Dewey draws radical implications from this simple thought when he denies the existence of "ends" in enterprises like education and morality. We are always "growing" in the sense that our habits and environments are in processes of change as long as we live. So our efforts at any given time ought to be geared toward making present activity more meaningful and rich. One way to do this is to acquire the habits necessary to construct deliberative events. Deliberative events, and the action plans included in them, function as ends-in-view. They mediate broken habits. Any attempt to frame our practical justifications in terms of ends held fixed is likely to distort some very basic facts about human life.

FIXED-END VIEW IN DISGUISE?

At this point, a sophisticated defender of FEJ is likely to challenge the pragmatist to show that her model of deliberative events is in fact notionally different than the fixed-end view. Imagine the following fixed-end reply: "Certainly, one need not believe in 'final ends' as goals beyond all action in order to believe in ends that are fixed relative to a particular piece of deliberation. The fixed-end structure of practical justification need not make the assumption that because some ends serve to justify conduct now, they must in all other circumstances. In what sense then is the pragmatist really dispensing with this justificatory structure, which seems so basic to our commonsense way of thinking of practical deliberation? Perhaps part of the problem is that you pragmatists exaggerate the implications of taking change seriously. Surely you must say something about which practical consideration [read: fixed end] justifies an action plan. Why not say that Addams' decision to found Hull House is justified because of certain ends taken as values (social service, shared cultural activities, etc.)? This is all that the fixed-end theory of justificatory structure must maintain."

The first point to make in response is that while the deliberative event is still incomplete, ends are *tools of analysis* for thinking about the situation. While the deliberative event unfolds, these ends do not play justificatory roles but rather furnish standpoints or perspectives for interpreting the situation.

After the deliberative event is completed, and the action plan appears to be a successful way of resolving the problem, Addams may well describe her decision by reference to ends that justified her action plan. However representations of the deliberative event that only refer to general ends will be shorthand descriptions of what could be described in greater detail. Addams' subtle writing performs just this needed detail.

To be sure, the fixed-end account of justificatory structure looks a little more plausible in much simpler cases, especially those in which some routine response to a certain kind of situation has been worked up over time. Whenever I have a headache, I take aspirin. I now have a headache. I have reason to take aspirin. But even such simple, routine procedures require some level of thought and interpretation, if only to make decisions about when and how to execute the plan. Moreover, two points should be kept in mind about routine procedures. First, there was some time when this procedure took hold. It may not have involved anything like a problem-solving event. However, it did involve acquiring habits keyed to certain kinds of situations—habits that involve an element of "know-how." Second, any such routine habit may fall prey to an unforeseen problematic situation and thus require the construction of a deliberative event. The fixed-end account of the structure of practical justification can serve to represent practical reasoning about a routine deliberative event, viz., a deliberative event that matches a regularly recurring type of situation, such as a headache. I will return to this point later.

This last point brings me to an important pragmatist claim about "means" and "ends." Dewey often says that means and ends are on a "continuum." He also denies that there are any ends-in-themselves or final ends. Part of what he means is that every completed deliberative event leads to new problems and new deliberations. You might take the "ends" of pragmatist practical reasoning to be *solved problems,* but solving one problem leads to new and unforeseen problems. In this respect, completed deliberative events are "ends" that function as means to yet new situations and new deliberative events. Setting up Hull House was but the beginning of a whole new set of challenges for Addams and her friends. Even the trivial act of eliminating a headache by taking a painkiller sets up a new situation: I can now focus on my reading for the day.

One might argue that pragmatism does commit to general ends that could be considered "fixed" relative to deliberations about more specific ends, such as Addams' "social service to the poor." These general ends might be called "continuous growth of meaning," or "continual resolution of problems." Why not concede that *these* ends are substantive justifiers that a pragmatist could insert into the fixed-end structure of justification?

In reply, note that these general pragmatist ends function as considerations that help us clarify the very nature of practical reason. Typically, these general ends are developed in response to very general, "theoretical" questions about the nature of practical reasoning. To say that "continuous growth" is an end or goal is in part the pragmatist's way of reminding us of the theoretical point that all ends of practical reason function in a concrete problematic situation that is always in some temporal flux. "Continuous growth" thus functions in a cautionary way, similar to the way that Rorty claims the truth predicate functions. Rorty argues that one "cautionary" pragmatist meaning of "truth" is that "'your belief that S is perfectly justified, but perhaps not true' [reminds us] that justification is relative to, and no better than, the beliefs cited as ground for S."[32] Analogously, to say that "an end is justified because it promotes *continuous growth*" is really just another way of saying, "Relative to current habits and circumstances, this end functions to bring harmony, but because things change, new habits might be needed for further growth."

Now, we can say that "problem resolution" is the "formal" end of *all* deliberative events. Deliberations aim at clearing up a problem by formulating an action plan. Nevertheless, it is incorrect to say that this is the end that *justifies* an action plan. Just as it would be vacuous to say that an explanation is a good explanation if it successfully accounts for the phenomenon, so too is it vacuous to say that an action plan is justified if it successfully resolves the problem. Insert "justified" for "successfully resolves the problem," and we have a very short circle indeed.

I have been replying to attempts to show that the pragmatist view is at base simply a restatement of the fixed-end account of justification. I believe that there is a real difference in the conceptual meaning of these views. In the next two sections, I will demonstrate the practical difference between the two views.

BETTER LEARNING THROUGH PRAGMATISM

The fixed-end view maintains that justificatory chains terminate in ends taken as values. How can it account for learning that some change in ends might be desirable? I suppose that a fixed-end defender could say something like, "Well, I see now that I have a *new* valued end that justifies some new action." But this of course does not answer the question of *why* this new end is a better idea than the old one.[33]

It might be objected that I am unfairly smuggling in a question whose answer can only be given in the context of a full-blown theory of justification. A defender of the fixed-end view might reply that the demand to give an account of learning about why a change is desirable requires a full theory of value. Hedonists may say, "I learned that I was not getting as much pleasure writing as I could running." Utilitarians may say, "I learned that I could better maximize happiness by serving Oxfam than by pursuing a career as a philosopher." A Kantian could say, "I learned that writing off that expense on my taxes amounts to making a special exception for myself, so I had better change my filing policy."

This objection is not well founded. Regardless of which full-blown theory of justification we adopt, we will still need to give some account of why an action plan Y fairs better than action plan Z with respect to the values of that justification theory. Either we say something like, "This action plan just does a better job than that one in satisfying the constraints of the justification theory (leaving aside any sense of why or how the plan so succeeds)," or we appeal to something like the pragmatic model of reasoning about problem cases.

Nevertheless, the pragmatist view of justificatory structure will not leave the full-blown accounts of justification unscathed. For the question can always be raised at the "higher" justificatory level, "How did you come to learn that maximizing good is the end that you should be looking toward here?" Or "How did you come to learn that your own maximal pleasure was the end that is proper to adopt over a life?" It seems plausible that the answer will be couched either in a pragmatic account of deliberative events or one in that gives no answer.[34]

A second argument related to learning is that the pragmatist model, when consciously adopted, promotes better learning. If we grant that life involves change, growth, and continuous activity, then it is better to frame our practical ends as provisional action plans—what Dewey calls "ends-in-view"—that are themselves embedded in deliberative events. Thinking of practical justification as based in fixed ends tends to promote a certain inflexibility in the face of change. It also tends to take us away from the context sensitivity sometimes needed when novel problems arise.

Jane Addams is a good case. She welcomes change. She is sensitive to the particular meanings of her own habits and those of her culture regarding treatment of the poor. Addams learns by being willing to change her ideas about what sort of pursuits are appropriate to an educated woman of some privilege. She is willing to experiment with a radical change in the kind of role a woman of her class is expected to play. For Addams, neither a domestic caregiver nor an autonomous professional woman, the Hull House project navigates to a new way. Addams gets to that new way, in part, by making use of habits that help learning.

These habits enable her to construct new deliberative events—
events that help her frame new situations as problems and move
to novel solutions for these problems.

CONTINUAL EVALUATION

Just as the fixed-end view does not adequately account for learning about why new ends should be adopted in favor of old ones,
it does not offer an adequate account of the continual reevaluation of ends over time. The historical transmission of habits means
that in a very real sense we who come later may participate in
the deliberation about the same social habits as those who came
before. Addams and those who worked with her may have left
out important factors in the way they framed their problematic
situation. Some have argued, for example, that Addams was not
critical enough of the traditional association of women with care-
giving. Further, we who come later will face new circumstances
that will require transforming these same historically transmitted
habits in novel ways unforeseen by Addams.

Pragmatists have been criticized for not defending some view
of the "ends" that ought to guide practical reasoning.[35] According to this complaint, Dewey's "instrumentalism" may have plenty
to say about means but nothing about ends. It simply accepts
whatever ends are given and tells us about how to realize those
ends effectively. In reply we must remember that ends-in-view
or action plans are never "finally fixed." It is not that action plans
are arbitrary; what is arbitrary is the judgment that we have de-
liberated enough to be sure that our plans are *terminally* justified.
Even after a plan is tested in action and appears to work toward
solving a problem, we cannot say for certain that the plan is justified. We might learn of a better way later on. After some time
we might see that what at first appeared to be a satisfactory result later proves unacceptable. If by the "end" of deliberation
we mean "action plan" or "end-in-view," then pragmatists maintain that no end can be accepted as "given" (if by "given" we
mean definitively justified).

Should we say that a deliberative event whose action plan
later proves to be inadequate was justified relative to the prior

situation *S1* but not relative to the later situation *S2*? Or should we say that we were wrong in believing that the previous action plan was justified? In other words, did we mistakenly think that the deliberative event was completed when in fact it really was (and is) open?

The answers to these questions depend upon our purposes and the nature of the problem at hand. Imagine a semifictional Jane Addams. She learns later that her own personal psychological crisis is not due to a sense of guilt and worthlessness in the face of the social problems of the poor. Rather, she learns that she has deep-seated psychoses tied to early childhood experiences. What at first appeared to be primarily a matter of guilt based on a sense of her social privilege is really more a matter of some repressed early childhood experience. The bullfight experience, which came to represent a feeling of being "tried and condemned, not only by this disgusting experience but by the entire moral situation which it revealed," was misinterpreted. Yes, she has become sensitive to real social problems, leading to a sense of responsibility for the plight of the poor. But there are other issues that she has left untouched by the Hull House action plan. If this is the case, I would be inclined to say that Addams had mistakenly framed the problem and the action plan addressing it. Thus, the deliberative event was not really completed.[36] In this case, it seems entirely appropriate to say that Addams has made a mistake about her problem because a very basic element of her indeterminate situation was left unaddressed.

Now consider another hypothetical case. It is years after Hull House has been founded. Addams comes to see that class oppression just seems to get worse and worse. Hull House was founded initially to foster a sense of unity between the classes. This goal of unity led Addams to run Hull House in as apolitically as possible. Experience of the brutality and the organized power of the capitalist class eventually leads Addams to the decision to use Hull House specifically for the purpose of militant organizing of the working class. She comes to see that Hull House has in fact been simply a way of coating the bitter pill of capitalism and not a real force for transforming the latter.

In this scenario, I would describe Addams' new action plan as addressing a new problem, not as invalidating the initial Hull House plan. Part of the reason this seems appropriate is that Hull House is not shown, in this scenario, to be a radically misguided experiment, but rather to need some modification in light of new and unforeseen circumstances. The deliberative event that was completed with the implementation of the action plan to found Hull House is still, by our best lights, justified. What has happened now seems to be best described as a new indeterminate situation.

The role that general ends play in justification, and the sense in which all action plans are fallible, can be fruitfully illuminated by pursuing the analogy between practical justification and the adequacy of scientific hypotheses. The first point to note is that practical reasoning and scientific reasoning are both, in a broad sense, abductive. Tyles points out that it might seem that an inference to a practical judgment is deductive, but the appearance is misleading. This is in part because in practical reasoning, "the inference to a means merely picks out one of several alternative ways to realize an end; it does not conform to the deductive model."[37] Recall our example:

(1) If one accepts social service as a value, then one should undertake to use one's time and energy to help others.
(2) Addams accepts social service as a value.
(3) Founding Hull House is an appropriate way for Addams to use her time and energy to help others.
(4) Addams should found Hull House.

One problem here is that the truth of the first three premises does not guarantee the truth of the conclusion because first, as Tyles points out, there are other possible means. One could believe that (1) is true, but not accept that (4) has to be true. For example, Addams might spend her time working in a special clinic for the poor. Second, (1) and (2) might be true, but they might conflict with other values at stake, such as Addams' responsibility for taking care of a sick family member. These observations are tied to our earlier point about the interpenetration of habits. Our lives are comprised of multiple habits that express multiple values. The assessment of our action plans requires sensitive attention to the many habits and goods that may be at stake.

Given that it makes sense to say that practical reasoning is abductive in something like the way that scientific explanations are, let's pursue the analogy a bit further by looking at hypotheses that explain particular events. Assume that three out of five people in a household fall ill, vomiting at roughly the same time. This event needs explanation: we are unclear exactly what the cause of this illness is or whether there is even any common cause. We consider competing hypotheses: the people became ill because they ate the same contaminated food; they became ill because they are suffering from the same virus, etc. General considerations come into play in the formation of these hypotheses. These consist of, among other things, general knowledge about food poisoning and viruses, including symptoms for each. We also have general knowledge of testing procedures for determining the presence of specific causes. One of our aims in adopting an explanatory hypothesis is to describe the situation or event adequately. Is this a situation of "people falling ill from food poisoning" or is it one of "people falling from stomach virus?" We can only be confident about a description after subjecting competing hypotheses to the relevant tests.

Now consider practical reasoning about what would be good to do. In a sense similar to reasoning about explanatory hypotheses, the practical reasoner attempts to describe her situation adequately. This begins in the second step of a deliberative event: a preliminary interpretation of the problem, including a view of what important goods and evils are at issue. Is this a situation of "not making use of one's talents for socially beneficial work," or is it a situation of "suffering from the return of repressed early childhood memories"? Or are both of these interpretations correct in some respects? As practical deliberation proceeds, people tend to get clearer and clearer about the nature of the situation. We might think of the various action plans considered as differing interpretations of the significance of the problem, the habits, and the situation. After an action plan is adopted and implemented, we can come to some decision about how to describe the case correctly.

The general considerations that constrain our choice of explanatory hypotheses are *normative* in the sense that they are regulative considerations that help make sense of aspects of the particular event to be explained. Similarly, an action plan and a representation of a deliberative event are constrained by general considerations. Action plans are justified not only by general considerations but also by the way in which acting on the plan resolves the particular problematic features of the case, especially the way the plan helps to realize particular goods and avoid particular evils.

Just as erroneous explanatory hypotheses are instructive, so too are erroneous action plans. From our mistakes we learn about both the particulars of the situation and the general items of knowledge brought to bear on the case. Scientific reasoning and good practical reasoning are self-corrective in the sense that the claims they produce are tested against experience. When they fail that test, we learn something.

THE TRUTH IN THE FIXED-END VIEW
OF PRACTICAL JUSTIFICATION

As I have mentioned, the fixed-end view does at least appear to express the form of practical reasoning about routine situations correctly. Just as we are sometimes relatively clear about what hypothesis explains an event, we may find ourselves relatively clear about what good to pursue because the situation is familiar. I am a teacher. Here are some papers to grade. I ought to grade them. Grading papers is such a routine part of teaching that the teacher usually has little, if any, difficulty in framing a practical justification. As long as we remember that even in these routine cases the action plans are fallible and that "ends alone" are not justifiers, it is somewhat acceptable to speak of "ends fixed relative to a piece of deliberation." These ends comprise part of the justificatory rationale for a routine decision. Consider now a

few such routine cases—routine in the sense that the deliberative event and action plan are relatively settled:

(1)   A person wants to make clear to another why she does what
she does. She says, "You don't understand why I had to leave
the party early. I had planned to leave at that time all along
because of an action plan that I now implement: grading papers. When you ask, I offer a brief justification of my action: I
had to get the papers done."

(2)   The person needs a reminder of commitments that she has
because she is acting somewhat irrationally. In response she
says, "I have already made the judgment that I would leave
the party by 7:30 PM. You know about that commitment. It
is now 9:30. You gently remind me by pointing out the end or
action plan that I really do have, but to which I fail to attend."

(3)   Sometimes people appear to be acting irrationally. In such instances it may be appropriate to offer a charitable explanation by appealing to possible reasons motivating the person:
"I wonder why a woman left the party suddenly. Is it because
of a prior engagement, or simply boredom?"

Notice that in these cases there is no problem in the sense of a
live question about what would be good to do in an indeterminate situation. The problems here have to do with interpreting
another's ends that, presumably, have resulted from prior deliberations.

I have argued that pragmatism provides a better account of
the structure of practical justification than does the fixed-end view.
My argument is not that the fixed-end view is a completely false
description. It is rather that the fixed-end account is too limited
and truncated; it distorts and misleads in ways that may hamper
good practical reasoning.

In concluding this discussion of practical justification, I want
to stress that the habits that make possible practical justification
are *norms* of conduct. This means, in part, that those equipped
with these norms have a sense of proper procedure and the ability to amend procedure in light of new problems. Put another
way, rational action, according to the pragmatic account, at least

in part involves the use of norms that make possible self-correction and self-control. In what follows, I will argue that we should not exaggerate the degree of self-control possible in any given instance. Given that norms or habits are functional transactions with complex environments, an individual person will only be able to do so much to directly control and modify habits.

Motivation: A Habit-Based Account

The claims in the previous section are basically epistemological in character. They are concerned with the nature of practical knowledge as it figures in intentional action and practical justification. I now turn to a discussion of the volitional dimension of practical life. Habits or norms are the components of a person's character. To have a character is to have a relatively well-integrated body of habits. This in turn is what is required to be an agent who can reliably "will" certain actions and results. To have a "character" is to have a pattern of desires and abilities to act, as much as it is to have a framework of practical knowledge for making judgments about conduct. Although we analytically distinguish the epistemological from the motivational, we should see that these two parts of practical life are intimately related. A small child lacks the ability to "will" a complicated life plan such as pursuing a scientific career because he or she does not have the requisite control over impulses or the requisite refinement of abilities and powers. But the child also lacks the powers of judgment and perception that result from years of work in a laboratory. In short, what we mean by "practical knowledge" is grasp of appropriate conduct in some practice or activity as well as ability to conduct oneself in accordance with such grasp. The point is that the grasping and the doing are interrelated.

The discussion that follows draws largely from Dewey's account of habits and will in *Human Nature and Conduct.* My criticisms of the fixed-end view of practical justification and intentional action are "Deweyan" in the sense that they are inspired by Dewey's views. Dewey blunts the radical nature of his pragmatic revision by not clearly indicating that he is offering an alternative account of *justificatory structure*. Dewey's criticisms tend to focus on good reasons to abandon conceptions of timeless, unchanging ends outside of all action. While his criticisms have merit, they don't touch the heart of the pragmatic revision indicated by his position. Therefore, the criticism of the fixed end view that I have offered goes somewhat beyond Dewey's presentation of his pragmatist criticism. In this section, however, I stick close to the main lines of his view of habits and will, because I do believe that it is correct.

HABITS AS SYSTEMS OF IMPULSIVE ENERGY

According to Dewey habits are, among other things, relatively organized systems of impulsive energy. The organization involves cognitive, volitional, and affective patterns. We have already discussed the ways in which habits interpenetrate. The point in connection to volition is that such interpenetration of many habits involves a kind of balance or harmony between many disparate elements. This balance can occur in the simple ability to carry on a conversation while eating dinner with appropriate table manners, or it can be achieved in a much more complicated way, as when Jane Addams manages to harmonize habits of "feminine care" with those of "professional advancement." Harmonies of habits involve the ability and energy to act in certain ways, given certain circumstances. Effective harmony of energies and impulses is one element of rational conduct. A requirement of rational action seems to be that a person does not let one impulse get the better of her thought and conduct. If, after founding Hull House, Addams was miserable—continually thinking of a career as doctor—we might say that she is not acting rationally insofar as she continually lives and works at Hull House without any effort to come to grips with this misery. Unreasonable conduct, in Dewey's view, often occurs when one impulse system dominates reflective thought, excluding adequate consideration of other impulses. Traditionally, moral philosophers have been interested in the kind of case in which "passion" overrules reason. Dewey does not describe this as a conflict among two *distinct kinds* of human faculties, reason and passion. The threat frequently described as irrational "passion" is better described as disruption of *relatively* disorganized impulses. So if Addams is so gripped with thoughts and desires about becoming a doctor that she begins to falter in her participation in Hull House, we might say that her imagined "passion" for a career as a doctor is an irrational irruption. She has to find a way to "master" this passion so that she can carry on her work. The solution may be radical. The obsession with being a doctor may indicate the need for a radical change in life plan, or it may require more remedial measures like counseling.

The conflict between organized and relatively disorganized impulse systems is only one case. We can find other cases in which the conflicts are between two or more relatively organized impulse systems. Sometimes, as Dewey points out, there is too much reflection, so that, for example, a person is inclined to be overly cerebral about his relationships with others. It may be accurate to say that he is too fond of reflective activities and misses out on more spontaneous sharing with other human beings. Consider, for example, a scientist who is so fond of his research that he is insensitive to the needs of friends or family members.

Perhaps a real example will help. Some years after World War II various participants in the Manhattan Project admitted to a sort of short-sightedness with respect to their rush to build the bomb in the summer of 1945. Some reported that before the surrender of Germany, people (reasonably) perceived that a bomb was urgently needed inasmuch as it was known through intelligence that German scientists were working toward creating an atomic weapon of their own. Once Germany surrendered, some scientists involved in the atomic weapon project headed by Oppenheimer in New Mexico reported a vague sense that the need for a bomb was not as urgent. Indeed Japan had not surrendered, but that seemed imminent. Nonetheless, there was no real discussion about whether the project ought to be continued. Afterwards, members reported that there was a kind of "inevitable" momentum to continue. This drive to continue was no doubt fueled by a variety of factors. The military had offered unlimited resources to support the project. The team had grown close, developing an esprit de corps as they worked. No doubt also the sheer desire for knowledge on the part of individuals whose lives were dedicated to such research furthered the momentum. Now, the lesson of this example is not necessarily to blame either the research team or the military fifty years after the fact (although, perhaps in some instances such blame may be legitimate). In fact, it might be that they could not have helped the way that they looked at matters at the time. Rather, the point here is the failure of members of the project to deliberate well was not due to reason becoming overruled by blind passions. Instead, what had happened was that certain habits and impulses connected to love of research, camaraderie, and concern about the war had taken shape under certain special conditions (i.e., the joining of military and research institutions) so as to lead to a failure to think through the consequences of the research thoroughly. The question for the Deweyan approach would be, "How can we change conditions in the military-cum-research institutions so as to prevent these kinds of shortsighted deliberations in the future?" Any number of solutions might suggest themselves (e.g., citizen review boards). In any case, the habit-based approach rules out simple solutions such as morally exhorting scientists "to work for the good" or "not to be so intellectual and cold—to try to be passionate and caring." In short, what is required is the reworking of a portion of the shared conduct of a certain group under certain conditions.

HABITS AND WILL

The failure of rationality in this case is a failure of *both* will and judgment. Habits were allowed to develop in directions that lead to complex epistemological and volitional patterns that might have been shaped in a different, more productive way. These habits are obviously highly refined expressions of complex psychic and social patterns. Habits are constituted out of ongoing more or less organized energy of an organism. So long as we are alive impulses drive us to respond to our environment. Once incorporated and mastered, habits provide the individual the power to act, and the knowledge of what kind of actions are appropriate. This point makes some sense of Dewey's somewhat startling remark at the end of the second chapter of *Human Nature and Conduct* that habits are *will*.[38] A human is comprised of a set of habits that "demand" certain sorts of responses to certain sorts of situations.

The claim that habits are will—or at least make sense of what it is to "will"—can be taken as an inference to a hypothesis that makes realistic sense of certain facts about human motivation. Dewey claims that many accounts of human willing amount to "magical thinking." The idea of such accounts is that through some sort of internal commands we can cause actions to occur. We tend to believe that by simply thinking to ourselves "I want to do x" we can straightaway accomplish x. The fixed-end view tends toward this picture of human willing and action. Here I am, an agent with purposes in thought. I "decide" that I want this end instead of that and set out to secure the end. But of course the only way I can achieve some end, say "being a master cook," is by *gradually* assimilating cooking habits. The point is not that a novice cook, musician, or painter cannot perform *some* of the actions characteristic of the activity (after all, even a novice trumpet player may occasionally hit a perfectly played note, indistinguishable from a virtuoso) but that novices cannot do so reliably with little effort and in ways that sustain the activity at its best, perhaps even advancing or modifying the character of the activity.

Of course the fixed-end theorist may concede that wishing alone is not sufficient for causing action and that some kind effective desire must be present as one among other factors that cause the action. But this leaves too much out of the story. To say that the desire and perhaps some appropriate belief "caused" the action does not inform us of the richer context that needs to be in place in order to generate action. It is like saying that in order for a garden to grow one must throw seeds in the ground and water occasionally. This much is true, but of course seeds, ground, and water do not a thriving garden make.

Dewey points out that a person who has bad posture obviously cannot simply change his posture by "willing in thought" to "stand up straight." He posits that "A man who does not stand properly forms a habit of standing improperly, a positive, forceful habit. The common implication that his mistake is merely negative, that he is simply failing to do the right thing, and that the failure can be made good by an order of will is absurd. One might as well suppose that the man who is a slave of whiskey-drinking is merely one who fails to drink water."[39] Shortly after this passage, Dewey warns us not to fall into the error of thinking of habits as dispositions of body, needing to be commanded or controlled by "mind." Dewey holds that the adequate conception of "good posture" can only be hit on after we have formed the habit of standing up straight. How, then, do I even begin to start standing up straight? I start by readjusting my stance, gradually, consciously. It is not that I do not even know how to stand or walk (I am not crippled, we shall assume); it is rather that I walk and stand badly. I utilize these rudimentary abilities in order to try to act differently. Perhaps I overcorrect for a while. Sometimes I get it right but cannot hold it in place. The same sort of process is true for all kinds of acquired abilities. I may not know how to sing well, but I do have the ability to talk, to vary the tone of my voice, and the like. These habits serve as the basic material with which I can start to develop my singing voice. We are constantly engaged in a process of readjusting habits, shedding old habits and acquiring new ones. However, this is never creation ex nihilo but rather a continuous transformation.

HABITS AS PROPULSIVE

Without habits we would have no "idea" or "purpose" to begin with. Dewey puts it this way:

> If we could form a correct idea without a correct habit, then possibly we could carry it out irrespective of habit. But a wish gets defi-

nite form only in connection with an idea, and an idea gets shape and consistency only when it has a habit back of it. Only when a man can already perform an act of standing up straight does he know what it is like to have a right posture and only then can he summon the idea required for proper execution. The act must come before the thought, and a habit before an ability to evoke the thought at will.[40]

Dewey goes on to make the point that in some cases—especially cases of "bad" habits—the thing to do is not to think of a desired end but to find some other concrete course of action to replace the bad habit. So, for example, the hard drinker would do well not merely to think of a future in which drinking is absent but to find some alternative activity that takes him away from the habit. Habits are *active* means that incorporate some objective environment in order to operate (e.g., among other things, I need ground, nourishment, and healthy limbs in order to sustain my habit of walking). In light of this observation, a change of environment is often the key to a change in habit. For example, the first thing a hard drinker may require is removal from the setting (e.g., friends, family) that has provided the context for the habit of drinking. A more complex example is a town that has been devastated by major job losses, which in turn lead to a lack of adequate financial support for the community. Under these conditions habits of the community may change in a way that leads to violence, anomie, and self-destructiveness. One might even argue that it would be irresponsible to sit in judgment on behaviors that develop under these conditions without attending to what is required to change them. Of course the Manhattan Project example mentioned earlier also demonstrates the complex way that environment and habits interact. The same is true of Jane Addams and Hull House. Addams' bullfight experience signaled a deep conflict in her habits and in her social world. The change that she found necessary was a change of environment—a change that involved a fairly radical new experiment in shared living.

These observations have important implications for what it means to make responsible judgments about others and what it means to share responsibility. Once we accept Dewey's account of habits, it is hard to accept the idea that moral failures are simply flaws in individual will or the result of bad social environments. We have a much more complex situation to deal with: habits involve both personal and social dimensions, and they cannot be changed through "wishes" or "acts of will." They can only be changed by tending to the complex confluence of conditions that they are in transaction with. Only careful study of these conditions can help determine who is responsible for moral failings and what needs to be done to correct them. We might think of responsibility here as adequate *responsiveness* to the swirl of interacting habits and environmental conditions. Each individual is charged with responsibility for this confluence of conditions. I *find* myself responsible. I cannot help but be embedded in a tangle of complex relationships to social, natural, and personal environments. Moreover, I alone cannot resolve flaws in personal or social habits. This requires cooperation with other people as well as environing conditions. Consider Dewey's comments on the responsive aspect to habits. "The essence of habit," he writes, "is an acquired predisposition to *ways* or modes of response, not to particular acts except as, under special conditions, these express a way of behaving. Habit means special sensitiveness or accessibility to certain classes of stimuli, standing predilections and aversions, rather than bare recurrence of specific acts. It means will."[41] Just prior to this passage, Dewey gives an example of a man who in a fit anger one time in his life kills another person. Even though this man is not a repeat murderer, Dewey maintains that his one-time act is a result of a habit—a predilection to anger that under special circumstances resulted in murder.

To say that habits are propulsive is not simply to say that they are forces that sometimes overtake us. They are, in a sense, always operative. Dewey points out that obviously habits such as "walking" or "talking" are not always overtly expressed in behavior. Nonetheless, someone who is able to use language has deeply internalized a certain way of dealing with the world that permeates conscious life. I "talk to myself." I see objects and automatically "name them." Someone who has the habit of walking is not always walking, but the habit is not passively waiting to be activated (e.g., it occurs in dreams). Habits that are not overtly expressed are potential energy that is temporarily suppressed by some other habits. So now I sit still as my habits of typing, writing, and reading take the fore of my attention, thus displacing the habit of walking that brought me here. The habits of walking to my computer, sitting down and typing at a certain time, getting up, and going home could all be characterized as a certain "work habit" that I have. This work habit does not have to take the form of the specific actions that I perform in walking to my computer at a certain time. This habit of work expresses itself in slightly different ways when the work at hand is teaching. It would of course be more appropriate to talk of my work habits (in the plural). These habits in turn interact with other habits—say certain recreational habits. In the broadest sense, all of my habits make my character—the overall way in which I conduct myself in all my various habits. Furthermore, the sort of character I have is heavily dependent on the sorts of social relations that I enter into—the sorts of conceptions of myself that I internalize from the standpoint of others. Thus the kind of work habit I develop is partly the result of the social groups with which I have interacted.

Character is a more or less integrated set of propulsive, interpenetrating habits. The more an individual's habits support, enhance, and reinforce each other, the more integrated the character. The more habits conflict with each other, the less integrated character. The structure of character is a *narrative* in two senses: it has a dramatic temporal structure, and the parts of character need to be interpreted in light of a larger context. Which features of this larger context are important for understanding any particular expression of character will depend on the kinds of questions we are interested in answering about ourselves or others. These patterns of habits that make up character can change as a result of our own self-corrective measures. But self-correction can be effectively accomplished only with the cooperation of our social and nonsocial environments.

2 | *The Goods in Activities*

Some Preliminary Points

Chapter 1 defended a pragmatist account of practical knowledge in the domains of intentional action and practical justification. This chapter extends the pragmatist view into a discussion of goods. I do not offer a full theory of value in the sense of a metaphysical account of the sources of values or an exhaustive enumeration of all values. My main objective is to explore the properties of goods that are revealed when we take seriously the centrality of habits to practical knowledge, as the latter figures in intentional action and practical justification. Habits, as we have seen, reside in practices and activities. For my purposes, the terms *norms* and *habits* may be used interchangeably. The virtue of using the term *norms* is that it connotes an element of "proper response," which is part and parcel of the Deweyan account of habits. Understanding norms or habits involves participating in norm-governed activity. This participation involves having a conception of oneself as a user of specific norms that express certain goods or values. We should understand "norm-governed activity" in a very broad way. This expression includes established practices and social roles such as "being a doctor" as well as relatively informal and spontaneous actions such as "giving a dollar to a homeless man."

My interest in this chapter is the way in which norm-governed activities are related to various kinds of values or goods. These activities include hiking, running, pottery, painting, cooking, feeding the poor, and helping people in need. Activities involve skills and character traits that are judged valuable as well. However, the range of things we call valuable seems to go beyond activities. It seems that we value the following: experiences like pleasure, states of affairs such as the most just world possible, relationships like friends and families, and things like rare works of art or natural objects.

I think an argument can be made that *activities* enjoy a kind of primacy in the sense that many, if not all, of the above items can be taken as short-hand references to complex activities. A relationship such as friendship involves a variety of activities like helping a friend in need, spending time with a friend, and so forth. A desirable state of affairs like "the most just world possible" is a world with particular activities such as the continuous fair distribution of social goods and opportunities. Even many experiential states are connected to activities required to realize them. Many of the distinctive kinds of aesthetic pleasures require deliberate effort to appreciate them, and sometimes to even bring them into existence. One might argue that even seemingly passive pleasures such as viewing a painting might require certain special ways of attending to the piece. The general point is that the existence of many valued experiences seems to involve deliberate "norm-governed activities." Obviously, though, this is not the case for all pleasures. We do enjoy random pleasures that just "happen" with little or no deliberate activities. Even though there may be various perceptual and cognitive habits involved in being sensitive to a beautiful sunset, the connection between these habits and the experiences that they produce does not usually seem to be direct.

Nonetheless, I will not attempt to give a complete answer to the question of what things deserve the predicate "good" or "valuable." Reduction of all of these items to "norm-governed activities" may not be possible. I don't think my general view in this chapter will be affected if that is the case. In any event, even if we can accomplish the reduction, we should not take this to imply "value monism." Norm-governed activities, and the values these realize, are irreducibly plural in nature and kind.

A Functional Account of "Good"

THE WARRANTING USE OF "GOOD"

Norm users acquire a sense of propriety when they acquire norms of thought and action. This sense of propriety involves being capable of determining the *relevance* of practical considerations. Among other things, having a sense of propriety in the use of norms involves understanding *why* some practical consideration is relevant for some good. Understanding why a practical consideration C is relevant involves understanding the role of C in realizing some *good*. In short, there is an internal connection between practical knowledge embodied in norms and judgments about the value of an activity. To know practically about an activity is to know what the activity is *good for*. An example will help. The person with practical knowledge of medicine understands the use of medical knowledge in judging particular cases—she can determine what considerations make certain facts relevant in particular cases. A good diagnosis involves careful attention to symptoms in the light of certain relevant theories about these cases. It further involves determining which practical responses are warranted in the light of the symptoms. But all of this presupposes a sense of what the facts and procedures are good for, namely the health and well-being of just this particular patient. The activities associated with good medical practice are not merely instrumental to some good external to them. These activities partly constitute good health. The doctor prescribes certain drugs and a certain dietary regime. Doctor and patient are involved in a shared enterprise directed toward the health and well-being of the patient. The doctor's norm-governed activities are "good for" the health of the patient in the sense that the rightful pursuit of these activities *partly constitutes* this end. The patient's right responses to the relevant practical considerations generated by a medical examination (e.g., proper diet and drug regime) are *in these circumstances* part of what it is for him to gain the good of health. The connection between the "practical knowledge" and the "valuation" is internal. To have practical knowledge is to be able to judge already what is a good and relevant practical consideration.

Another example may serve. Good trumpet playing results in certain aesthetic pleasures for player and listener. But these aesthetic pleasures are not added to the playing itself. They are "in" the playing, in the sense that without this particular norm-governed activity one would not be able to get just these pleasures of well-played trumpet. The trumpet player develops an appreciation for well-played trumpet *in* the playing. Furthermore, the example shows how wrong it is to construe norm-governed activity as rote mechanical response. Trumpet improvisation is norm-governed in that it is constrained by certain general rules with wide scope (e.g., playing with the chord changes, at the appropriate tempo, in the spirit of the song's mood and so on), but it is not the repetition of some predetermined pattern.

A. E. Murphy, whose account has influenced my own, develops the concept of what he calls the "justifying use of good."[1] When "good" is used as a "warranting" claim—a claim that something is worth pursuing or doing—we appeal to *reasons*, or grounds for, our judgment. These grounds are, in Murphy's account, embedded in our knowledge of the relevance of certain practical considerations for some end that is connected to some shared enterprise. The example he uses is skill in grading papers. The ability to judge a good paper is inextricably bound up with knowledge of the ends of the educational enterprise. I may find other reasons for judging a paper to be good: it gives me some spare scrap paper, it is funny, it is a concise statement of a person's emotional reaction to some social issue. But these considerations are not relevant for the judgment "good paper," when the purpose of the assignment was to test and develop a student's ability to think critically. Being able to grade well, to make well-founded decisions about what counts as a good paper, requires an understanding of the purpose of paper writing in the educational enterprise. When called on to explain or justify why a given paper is "good" (deserving of an "A"), a teacher will cite any number of considerations relevant to the immediate goal of writing a critical paper. These might be the fact that the paper clearly states a thesis, that it offers reasons for believing this claim, that it offers some reasons for believing the reasons, that it replies to possible objections, and so on. "Why are these considerations relevant?" it might be asked. Because the goal of the assignment was to foster critical thinking skills, and this sample of writing displays those skills. The paper is "good for" the development of these skills, not in the sense that it is instrumental to some end beyond it, but rather in the sense that this paper *expresses* this good of critical thinking. More precisely, the writing of this paper, in the context of a cooperative educational enterprise with teachers and other students, is an activity that realizes particular goods associated with critical thinking. Why is critical thinking a good? Because the development of this skill is part of the end of this educational enterprise in which I as teacher and my students are jointly engaged in. My deliberations in grading are, at their best, guided by these ends, not in the sense that I must always be entertaining these ends but in the sense that through my participation in the norm-governed activity of education I come to be able to appreciate and recognize the goods internal to this activity. But why, it might further be asked, are these ends of education worth pursuing? The training received in a college education is itself an integral means to other important human forms of life. It is important to a vital democratic society that citizens be able to exercise their critical faculties. It is important, obviously, to have a certain level of knowledge and understanding prior to participation in many careers. In short, the goods realized in the educational enterprise are themselves "good for"—in the sense of being an integral part of—other important activities. The general conclusion to draw here is that norm-governed activities, and the practical knowledge that these involve, are internally connected to the realization of certain kinds of goods. These goods are internally connected to certain activities in the sense that they could not be realized without the practical knowledge and participation in these activities.

My account of the "warranting use of 'good'" is in many respects an example of what Scanlon calls "buck-passing" accounts of "good."[2] It is "buck-passing" in the sense that the use of the predicate "good" occurs in an evaluative judgment, and this judgment is supported by properties *other than* "goodness" as such.

As Scanlon puts it, "Being good, or valuable, is not a property that provides a reason to respond to a thing in certain ways. Rather, to be good or valuable is to have *other* properties which constitute such reasons."[3] When we are called on to justify some practical judgment like "this is a good paper," we appeal to properties of the paper such as the fact that it clearly formulates a thesis, supports the thesis with an argument, and so forth. We should not think that when these properties are present, they are accompanied by a nonnatural simple property "goodness," which is the grounds for a positive evaluation of the paper. "Good" functions as a kind of place-holder in a judgment that is the conclusion of a piece of practical reasoning.

G. E. Moore famously challenged all "naturalist" accounts of value on the grounds that if one tried to define "goodness" in terms of some natural property like "pleasure," one can always meaningfully raise the question of whether the natural property is itself good. If "good" were in fact definable in terms of the natural property, we should not be able to ask this question. Thus "good" must refer to some simple, nonnatural property. Scanlon points out that Moore's open question argument can be addressed in the following way.[4] The reason we can always ask whether some natural property is good is that we can always ask whether the natural property at issue is in fact relevant grounds for the practical judgment. The fact that Moore's question seems valid shows not that "goodness" is a simple nonnatural property but that it is not anything like a property at all. It is rather a place-holder that plays a role in a piece of practical reasoning. As Scanlon says of the properties that provide grounds for a value judgment, "Just saying that something has these properties does not involve drawing it (the practical conclusion that they are grounds for the evaluation that some *x* is good)."[5] Buck-passing accounts of good do not, therefore, claim that the natural properties *analytically* define "goodness."

I would put the point like this. The judgment that "*x* is good" figures in an action plan that is warranted in the light of some set of natural properties (together with the entire deliberative event that sets the context for the judgment). Thus when "good" functions as a predicate in some practical conclusion it *could not* analytically mean some natural property like "pleasure." When we are dealing with the "warranting use of 'good,'" the best that we can do in treating the general meaning of "good" is to specify the functional role that the term plays in action plans and deliberative events. This functional role could be identified as "an action plan that is taken to be warranted in the light of those natural properties thought relevant to resolving some problem." It should be clear that this complex description of the functional meaning of "good" does not refer to a natural property claimed to be the analytic meaning of "good." The "property" that this complex description refers to is a functional one. That is, "good" plays the role in a conclusion of an inference about what to do, given certain circumstances that include certain salient natural properties.[6] For example, given the particulars of my situation, the city of Chicago may have certain properties that support the judgment that "it would be good to live there." "Good," in this context, applies to the action plan regarding the appropriateness of living in Chicago. It seems to me that we could substitute "good" for "appropriate" in many cases of "action plan *P* is appropriate."

Some may object on the grounds that we use "good" in plenty of cases that are not action guiding in any recognizable way. Consider value judgments about a person's character, about a tragic event that happened a century ago, about a beautiful person, or about a work of art. These kinds of judgments may imply certain kinds of actions, but why think that they always do?

In many such cases the value judgment may have little significant import for action, but something like an action plan may be involved. Works of art considered beautiful may be judged worthy of repeated visits to a museum or purchase of such a work. I may make it a policy to remind people of good character how much they are appreciated. Historical tragedies may serve as examples in a lesson on tragedy. At the very least, a judgment that "*x* is good" almost always involves some sense of the ways in which it is appropriate to respond to *x*. This is not simply the trivial claim that every value judgment involves uttering the words or thinking silently to oneself, "I think this is good." Rather, the point is that the expression of our evaluations is often as important as the content of our evaluations (more on this shortly).

Nonetheless, we must grant that "good," as a predicate in a practical conclusion indicating appropriate response, does not exhaust the use of the term. The natural properties claimed to be relevant for a certain judgment "*x* is good" themselves occur in the context of norm-governed activities that express certain values or goods. In short, the judgment that certain properties are *relevant* for a judgment that "*x* is good" presupposes some sense of *why* these are relevant. This point is evident in our example of grading papers. A paper is judged good relative to a larger context of activity in which grading plays a role. To have some sense of why these are relevant is to have some sense of the good of the properties—at least their good "here." We do not make value judgments in a vacuum. Norm-users are "always already" participating in a variety of activities and practices that embody and promote a variety of goods. When we call these activities and practices "good," are we identifying good with some natural property? I would answer thus: evaluation and understanding are bound together. Understanding the nature of human activities and practices involves understanding the values that these serve. This is part of what the grading example shows: understanding the practice of grading involves appreciating the educational goods served by the practice.

Thus, in addition to a functional account of "good" as a predicate in a practical conclusion of a deliberation, we have another use of "good" that picks out those particular values or goods expressed by norm-governed activities. In this second sense, "good" functions as an abstract label for a disparate variety of particular valuable activities. The functional definition of "good" as "whatever properties make activities worth pursuing" is the justification for applying the predicate "good" to these disparate activities. This functional definition is like the one just offered for the use of "good" in a practical conclusion. It is a second-order formal property that picks out other first-order properties. We need to inspect these first-order properties before we can say anything meaningful about the good of a particular activity. Similarly, we need to inspect the particular first-order properties that are alleged to ground a practical judgment that some action plan embedding a judgment of good is correct.

In this section I develop a more detailed view of the second sense of "good" as those particular values internal to norm-governed activities. Goods internal to an activity are goods that cannot be characterized independently of the norm-governed activity itself. Alasdair MacIntyre characterizes goods internal to a *practice* in this sort of way. He adds that one can only appreciate or "identify" these goods internal to a practice by participating in the practice.[7] He contrasts internal goods with goods "external" to a practice, those that are contingently connected to the practice. To take MacIntyre's example of teaching a child to play chess, to the extent the child's motivation to perform well is to win money he has every reason to cheat when he can. The "good" of money is contingently connected with the game of chess inasmuch as one could get money some other way than through playing just this game, or one could get it by violating the rules through cheating. However, to the extent that one participates in a game of chess for "the achievement of a certain highly particular kind of analytical skill, strategic imagination and competitive intensity, [one acquires] a new set of reasons, reasons now not just for winning on a particular occasion, but for trying to excel in whatever way the game of chess demands."[8] One may question the coherence of the distinction between "internal" and "external" goods because it would seem that some of the things called "goods internal to the game of chess" could in fact be characterized independently of these activities, namely, in terms of *other* activities that exemplify the same goods. But the fact that some goods *G1* ... *G*n may be internally connected to two different activities (say, chess and some complex computer game) is compatible with the claim that there is a distinction between internal and external goods for a given activity. We may say that

G1 . . . *Gn* are internally connected to activities *A1* and *A2* as long as we are not claiming that *G1* . . . *Gn* can *only* be characterized by *A1* or *A2* (but not in both). We could further explain the internal connection between some set of goods and some set of activities by pointing to properties shared by the activities (e.g., these are all intellectual, competitive games). The other thing we might try to demonstrate in a particular example is how a good like "strategic imagination" as exemplified in chess is different than its use in some other similar games.

MacIntyre's distinction between internal and external goods brings out the importance of the *valuational* dimension of human goods. By "valuation" I mean to include various *affective* and *volitional* phenomena, such as appreciations, enjoyments, pleasures, desires, and satisfactions. The pursuit of internal goods involves the cultivation of appreciation. The person who decides to take up the study of the trumpet is inspired by an appreciation of the unique aesthetic goods that are internal to trumpet playing. Of course, in some instances a person may joylessly take up trumpet, perhaps to please a parent or to meet people. In such cases the enjoyments and satisfactions to which trumpet playing may be instrumental are "external" to the activity of playing a trumpet insofar as other means would be adopted if they were more convenient or efficient. However, the existence of these degenerate cases does not impugn the general claim that *appreciating the values* of an activity requires participation in, or intimate familiarity with, the activity.

There are cases in which the means used in an activity *can only be* "externally" connected to the valued end. This is so, Dewey points out, in the case of coerced labor.[9] The laborer uses a factory job as a means to the end of earning a living wage but not for any enjoyment of value in the "work itself." He could just as well use his abstract labor power for a job fitting widgets as he could sorting linen. Work is chosen here because of the enforced necessity of obtaining the basic means to survive. Work is, we might say, more like an arbitrary "causal condition" for producing some external consequence than it is like an art chosen for inherent enjoyment and goods internally realized in the activity.

Although there are cases in which means and ends are externally connected, these are a degenerate class. We recognize the degenerate cases because we recognize other cases in which means are enjoyed as a meaningful constituent of ends. In this example, human needs, and the means of their satisfaction, are structured by the system of production under capitalism. This system of labor may not realize goods internal to its practice because of the way in which social practices are organized. Solving this problem requires changing the character of productive labor and is not simply a matter of "changing attitudes."

NONCOGNITIVIST AND FIXED-END SPECTERS

At this point, the following objection may be raised: "You emphasize the way in which participation in activities is internally connected to certain goods. You then point out that appreciation and enjoyment of these goods requires participation in activities. Grant these points. Is it not true that the 'value' or 'good' of an activity is not really 'in' the activity (as well as those objects used and produced in the activity)? Isn't the 'value' or 'good' in our pro-attitudes, standing desires, enjoyments and the like? After all, grading papers, playing trumpets, and playing chess are only good relative to agents who care about them. As such, the valuations made are simply expressions of what 'pleases us' and not what is in the 'world.'" This objection represents noncognitivist accounts of value judgments. What matters for our purposes now is not a particular formulation of this view but the general challenge issued to the pragmatist theory of practical knowledge and valuation.

It is one thing to claim that there would be no goods if there were no beings who cared about certain activities. It is quite another thing to claim that what it is for an activity to *be* good is that it satisfies the desires of an agent or that it is endorsed or cared about by the agent. I grant the former, but deny the latter. The first thing to note is that if we take seriously the notion of an "internal good," this latter explains the valuational attitudes of agents, and therefore it is conceptually more basic than these attitudes. That is to say, the appreciation of the goods internal to, for example, a game like chess is based on their being goods internal to this activity that explain the appreciation.

Secondly, *the ways* in which an activity is appreciated or enjoyed—the ways in which the activity is cared for—differ according to the nature of the activity and its internal goods.[10] We can only explain why it is appropriate to care for, or appreciate, an activity in a certain way on the basis of some more basic conception of the goods internal to an activity. For example, the fact that we judge it inappropriate for teachers to care about their students in certain respects (e.g., to care for their intimate life) reflects the fact that we include only certain kinds of appreciation as appropriate in this practical setting. The fact that a chess player may care about playing and winning simply to get money shows that his appreciation of chess is not appropriately grounded in appreciation of the distinctive goods of the game. It is possible to be in a family, to know what it means to be a family member, and yet not care about or appreciate this way of life. But we recognize this kind of case as degenerate because it is part of our conception of good family life that such life involves appropriate emotional and volitional responses. These evaluative responses are not simply external, contingent "additions" to the activities of a family life. They are required for the right living of such a life. These examples show that although emotive attitudes are integral to the values of certain activities, these are not arbitrary "additions" to the activity. Certain ways of caring about the activity are appropriate, and these ways are explained by our conception of the goods internal to the activity. True, there would be no goods "in" education, family, and games if no one cared about them. However, the way in which they are cared about is circumscribed by the nature of the purposes and ends of the activity.

Even after these points about appreciation are granted, some philosophers may still protest, claiming that we have yet to show that "goodness" exists as an objective property because "objectivity" is connected with a human independent realm. So now the objection is that the notion of "goods internal to an activity" is still not "objective" because these goods "exist" only in relation to human practice and activity. But what is the force of this objection anyway? There seems to be a deep-seated philosophical prejudice against ascribing the predicate "objective" to things human centered. Unless we are in the grip of a certain picture of what objectivity must be like, we should not be bothered by this worry. It is true that the notion of internal goods is relative to human practice. For some reason, conceding that the property of "goodness" is so relative strikes many philosophers as somehow demoting. But it is a consequence of my view of the internal connection between norms and goods that these latter admit of judgments about "right and wrong." There are "right" ways of pursuing health, chess games, the education of a child and so on, where "right" is relative to the goods internal to an activity. This is not to deny that deliberation in particular cases will be easy or infallible.

One final objection requires consideration in this section. The fixed-end theorist will try to argue in this way: "I will grant you that it is important to distinguish between internal and external goods. I will further grant the idea that norm-governed activities are internally connected to the realization of goods—that internal goods are constituted by norm-governed activities and are not additions to these activities. Nevertheless, all of this is quite compatible with the view that there is a plurality of fixed intrinsic goods that must be 'valued in themselves' in any practical deliberation. True, there may be many of these goods. True, these goods are constituted by norm-governed activities. But nonetheless, these goods are the 'fixed points' that any piece of practical deliberation must take for granted. At this point, the regress argument may be used. After all, shouldn't we admit that in any bit of practical deliberation there is some good valued in itself on pain of a regress of 'goods that are good for . . . ?' "

This important objection can be answered according to two different lines of argument. One line argues that the idea that our deliberations are guided by fixed goods is at best appropriate for a narrow range of deliberations, and even for this range, the model distorts important features of deliberation. Essentially, this argument mirrors the claim that I made in Chapter 1 about routine deliberation: the fixed-end account of practical justification captures at best cases of routine deliberation. The second line of argument involves showing that *in general* what explains the importance of goods is their integral *relations* to central areas of human life. As such, the use of the notion of an "internal good" is not to be taken as an unanalyzed simple that explains the choices of deliberation. It is rather a complex notion in the sense that what explains the importance of an internal good is its relations to other things. These two lines are related insofar as generalizations about the importance of internal goods arise out of particular deliberations, and particular deliberations are guided by examination of the relations into which the pursuit of a good will take us. Let's turn first to goods *in general*.

Goods in Relations

GOODS IN GENERAL

We have already seen that when we are concerned with the "warranting use" of "good" in our judgments, we appeal to considerations judged relevant relative to the particular purposes and goals of an activity. That this is a "good" paper is a warranted judgment on the basis of considerations relevant to this determination. The relevant considerations have to do with what the paper is "good for." In this case the paper is good for accomplishing certain aims of an academic course, which course is itself "good for" certain goals of the educational institution, which goals are themselves integral or "good for" promoting a vital democratic citizenry (among other things). Now, here we confront the fixed-end theorist directly. Such a theorist will be impressed by the chain of "good fors." Here someone gripped by the regress argument will point out that these "good fors," beginning with the particular paper graded "good," must eventually reach some intrinsic value good in itself. Such a value will explain why it is that the writing and grading of a certain kind of paper are "good." This good might be, for example, "skill in critical thinking" or a certain kind of "intrinsically valuable knowledge."

One problem with the intrinsic value account is that it does not explain why the pursuit of some goods is *more important* than that of others. The reason goods that are realized in an educational institution are important is that they are integral to sustaining and enhancing a variety of important areas of human life. Determining the overall importance of the goods internal to educational institutions is a matter of exploring the relations of these goods to other important things in human life.

In his *Moral Relevance and Moral Conflict,* James D. Wallace argues for just this view that the importance of a value consists in its relations to a variety of other things in human life.[11] We may hold that scratching itches (Wallace's example), feeling a cool breeze, dipping one's hand in warm water after a long walk on a blustery winter day, and a laugh at an absurd joke, are all valued "for themselves." However, typically these are not important goods. That is not to deny that *on certain occasions* they may be important in some way. For example, a laugh at an absurd joke may come after the culmination of some trial or tribulation. The feeling of a warm breeze may mark the culmination of an aesthetic experience. Typically, knowledge, friendship, and artistry (and the goods internal to them) are important or basic human values because of their central role in supporting and enhancing a variety of relations in human life. The ability to laugh at an absurd joke might not in itself amount to much. Appreciating this value, being able to engage in activities that "realize" absurd joke telling, is not something we characterize as a worthy vocation to which a life should be devoted. There are exceptions to this, such as great entertainers who master the art of joke telling, for example, but these exceptions can be accounted for by the fact that such joke tellers are skilled in some other important activity, such as acting or performing, that is itself an important value. To take another example, a joke told to cheer up a despondent friend may be an important part of what it is to be a good friend. In this case, the ability to appreciate and express an absurd joke is valuable within the context of a more fundamental value: friendship.

To return to Wallace's basic point, the importance of a value is a function of its connections to a variety of things in human life. Of theoretical knowledge, for example, Wallace claims, "The value of human knowledge derives from—that is, is explained by—its enabling supporting, sustaining, advancing, and intensifying other things in human life. . . . [W]e might mention among these other things, aesthetic experience, play, sociability (friendship), practical reasonableness (including morality), and religion. It is the relations of knowledge to these other things that make major fields of inquiry and study interesting and worth devoting a life to."[12] Knowledge partly constitutes many activities and practices. One cannot be a friend unless one has some basic knowledge about human needs, emotions, and interests in general, as well as knowledge of how these apply to a particular person. One could not be reasonable with respect to practical matters (such as morality) if one did not have some knowledge (e.g., what acts hurt people).

This *relational* account offers a general explanation of why certain goods are *typically* important. Wallace's argument is that the importance of a value is not adequately accounted for by the "intrinsicality" of the value. This is apparent when we consider why some intrinsic values (e.g., itch scratching) are not considered important or basic human goods. We now turn to a discussion of deliberation about particular goods.

GOODS IN PARTICULAR

The fixed-end theorist may at this point attempt to concede that what explains *in general* the importance of a value is its interconnections with important areas of human life yet claim that in our particular deliberations we are not typically focused on such relations. That is to say, when I deliberate about matters such as grading, what medicines to prescribe a patient, and the like, I need not reflect on the larger role of "education" or "health" in human life in general. I simply have my goods "in view" and work to obtain them as efficiently as I can. This leads to the second line of argument against the fixed-end view of intrinsic goods. My argument is that there are indeed cases in which we simply have some "simple good" in view. But these are not the only or most important kinds of deliberation. Further, we should by now suspect that this picture distorts the complicated interconnections between activities and the plurality of goods in them.

There is truth in the idea that our "ends-in-view" in any particular piece of deliberation only capture a slice of the totality of relations that a particular activity bears to the larger whole of conduct. Recall our model of a deliberative event. Action plans mediate particular habits. Action plans do not, nor can they, deal with all habits. Good planning takes account of the fact that plans are subject to continual modification and revision in light of concrete experiences. Deliberation's goods— internal and external— are *particular*. The generalized ends that we may formulate through experience are clarifying instruments that we can use to judge the concrete particulars of the situation. The claim that many goods are internal to norm-governed activities does not imply that these activities are fixed. They are subject to change and revision as the conditions of their practice change and as they conflict with each other. Good deliberation involves being sensitive to the various goods at stake in some situation, especially when they conflict or become problematic. This suggests the quite plausible claim that what we take to be goods—the ends we consciously pursue—may turn out to be misguided. Straightforwardly, we can distinguish between the plans or aims of deliberators and the actual results of the activities of deliberators.

It may be that deliberators are sometimes only concerned with some one "good" held "fixed." Yet the fact that a person may consciously attend only to some one fixed good does not mean that *in fact* no other goods are involved in his activity. Secondly, goods require specification and as such are never simply given as general ends. Let's look at the first point by considering some of the possible permutations of the ways in which there may be mismatches between the conscious aims of deliberators and the various goods realized.

First, many activities can be pursued with awareness and appreciation of only a subset of internal goods. For example, a doctor might only be interested in the knowledge and skill gained through the performance of complicated brain surgery. It is not that she does not care about the health of her patients. It is rather that this does not figure largely in her conception of her professional activity. She views patients more or less as opportunities to better her technical skill and knowledge. Now, in such a case, criticism is warranted on the grounds that part of our conception of the practice of medicine is that practitioners show a certain regard for their clients. But the fact that a particular doctor fails to adopt concerned attitudes toward patients does not imply that patients are not benefited by her practice. After all, irrespective of the doctor's particular attitudes, to the extent that she successfully performs operations, her patients' health is in fact benefited. The general point here is that a person may concern herself with far fewer internal goods than those actually involved in an activity. The example illustrates how this could reflect negatively on a person. But it need not for the simple reason that oftentimes that part of an activity that can and should be reflectively considered is only a portion of the whole. For example, a doctor may really care about her patient's well-being, but her focus is (and should be) on the matter at hand (e.g., the body being operated on).

Nevertheless, a plausible ideal for the practical reasoner to strive for is continual awareness of the full range of internal goods. Of course, someone may not care about some of these goods. But what of that? The point is that the end consciously entertained during the pursuit of an activity may only reflect some subset of the internal goods involved with the activity. The fact that this may turn out to be so in some cases does not imply that the goods not cared about are not genuine goods objectively connected to the actual performance of the activity.

A second range of cases are those in which a person may simply perform an activity for some external good that results from it. For example, a doctor may pursue a career of medicine simply for fame and money. We will want to criticize such a person because he fails in some important way to express attitudes appropriate to the activity. Moreover, it is likely that someone who is constantly focused on such external goods will end up either failing in the activity in some way, thereby undermining his ability to get those external goods, or he will fail in some other area of human life (e.g., such a person motivated by external goods like fame and money is likely not to be a good friend or family member).

Thirdly, it is possible that someone carefully attend to an activity and its internal goods but fail to consider the activity's impact on other activities and their internal goods. The Manhattan Project example discussed earlier fits this sort of case as well as do other scientific research projects. We need not conclude that scientists themselves must always be focused on, or aware of, other social implications of their work. However, we should expect that this profession (as others) has some internal mechanisms of self-regulation. Moreover, one is never just a "scientist" or "business person." One is always this and more (a citizen, family member, religious believer, etc.). Thus, it is reasonable to expect that advocates of a particular activity or practice be sensitive to other areas of human life.[13]

These examples show that the ends of conscious deliberation never encompass all of the effects and conditions of a line of activity. An end-in-view, as Dewey calls it, is a conscious plan formulated to coordinate conduct. It is no fatal flaw that an end-in-view does not include within it every possible or likely consequence of an action.

The idea that the success or reasonableness of practical deliberation can only be assessed in light of some end held fixed "outside" the deliberations represents at best only the deliberation of a person who ignores the larger setting of her activity. She may well fix on some one good in an activity and simply care about how to realize it most efficiently. It does not follow, though, either that other goods are not in fact (internally and externally) related to her pursuit of some end or that this sort of fixed-end deliberation represents the only or most important kind of deliberation. The fixed-end account distorts the nature of that case in which someone is only concerned about getting one sort of good because it abstracts from the concrete context of other activities or other goods at stake.

The second argument against the fixed-end view of value—as an account of deliberation about particular goods—is that even when a single end is our concern, we nonetheless must still *specify* this end in order to determine what counts as the good in particular. To be sure we can say general things about goods. But when we are faced with a need to judge just what is good—what is of value in particular situations—this general knowledge can only serve to orient our judgments about what is good *here—in particular*. We may know what end in general it is appropriate to pursue (e.g., I am a doctor and the health of my patients is the end that I am working toward). But even when this general end is given, we still need to specify the good. When a doctor is concerned with judging what would be good for a patient she is concerned with "health for this person." This may mean a certain kind of exercise regime and diet. In regard to his definition of moral virtue as a mean between extremes, Aristotle is careful to qualify his statement so as not to imply that he has in mind a fixed numerical notion of mean but rather that of a mean that is "relative to us . . . and is not the same for everyone."[14] He gives an example of a wrestler called Milo. What counts as an adequate diet for the maintenance of health in Milo will be quite different from that of a less active, smaller person. Once we grant that ends require specification in terms of the particular circumstances, it is plausible to conclude that such end specification should change. What "health" means for an individual changes as she changes. An appropriate diet for a twenty-five-year-old may be quite different from that for a fifty-five-year-old with high blood pressure. These commonplace facts suggest that it is rarely (if ever) the case that we can assess our practical deliberation by some general end held "fixed." We deliberate about some general end as it is specified. And "specification" is a matter of what Aristotle calls "perception of the particular."

The idea of "specifying the good" can make sense of the following, rather striking passage by Dewey: "In quality, good is never twice alike. It never copies itself. It is new every morning, fresh every evening. It is unique in its every presentation. For it marks the resolution of a distinctive complication of competing habit and impulses which can never repeat itself. Only with a habit rigid to the point of immobility could exactly the same good recur twice. And with such rigid routines the same good does not after all recur, for it does not even occur."[15] But how particular can goods be? If a good bears absolutely no repeatable features, it is difficult to understand how it could be reidentified over time. What could such a thing be? Furthermore, it might be objected that the point about "end specification" does not involve anything like nonrepeatable features. After all, even if there is in fact only one Milo the wrestler requiring just this particular diet, we can still list the properties or features of Milo in a form such as "If there were to be another with features $F1 \ldots Fn$, then this person should have a health regime with features $G1 \ldots Gn$." Here we have a universal statement even though perhaps as a matter of contingent fact there was only one individual who fit the description.

The objection misses the point of Dewey's remarks. First of all Dewey's claim is that in *quality* the good is never twice alike. "Quality" might suggest something like "property" or "feature." But the context of our discussion suggests another interpretation. Dewey need not deny that we are guided by "universal" properties in specifying the good. A better way of taking his claim about the uniqueness of good is that even though habits or norms are repeatable features of agents, given the fact of change, they always have only *relative* stability. Habits that serve particular values are never perfectly repeatable. Each exemplification of them involves some degree of novelty—we never have a complete lock on goods.

In *Experience and Nature* Dewey points out that, interestingly enough, we do not speak of a problem of "goods." We take the latter for granted as natural or fitting, whereas evil or bad fortune marks a deviance from the way things ought to be. Sometimes we view evil as a "deserved bad," delivered by divine force or fate. What seems to be a more reasonable view of "goods" and "bads" is that they are explained by the fact that existence is partly stable and partly precarious. We would not deliberate about goods if there were no question about whether and how to realize them. A good previously sustained by supporting conditions (including our habits and impulses) may fail tomorrow as those conditions change. This seems to be Frederick Will's point about norms: "Norms," he says, "are explicitly socio-psychological entities. And they are by no means inert. In their aspects as features—and sometimes very basic features—of various spheres of life, they are typically, and always at least to some degree, in dynamic relation with other features of life, including other norms, in consequence of which they are liable to alteration both in respect to the conditions under which they are properly applied and to the character of the responses that are proper to their application." Will goes on to claim that this way of viewing norms sees them as open, as never completely defined in their manifest (or propositional) aspect. He then claims that "Speaking of norms as open (not closed) and as alive (not inert) is a mildly metaphorical way of calling attention to aspects of them that are essential for understanding both stability and change (and stability in change) in them, and also for understanding the way in which reflection, philosophical or otherwise, can perform a critical function upon them."[16] In short, we come to situations equipped with norms whose functioning enables some stability in conduct, including stability in goods or values. The most important of these goods will be those that have proved themselves to be basic for supporting and enhancing various forms of life—a claim that we made in the previous section regarding goods in general. Nonetheless, goods are particular in the sense that they are the result of a unique conflux of habits and impulses as they function under specific conditions.

So far as "goods" are the result of the more or less deliberate attempt to modify conduct, we can think of them as the products of norm-governed judgments or interpretations of a situation. But to say "norm-governed" here does not necessarily imply that the pursuit of goods involves highly reflective deliberation. It may in particularly problematic cases. But in other instances the interpretive use of norms is more or less nonreflective. Being educated in norms of action involves cultivating an appreciation for relevant considerations in certain practical contexts, and this cultivation often results in highly refined, unimpeded "performances." This cultivated ability is learned through practice— through doing. I may know a particular piece of music so well that I no longer need to practice it or subject it to evaluative scrutiny. The "good" of a well-played piece of music is the result of a highly refined ability to engage in this activity. In this sort of case it may not be completely appropriate to speak of a "judgment or deliberation about some good" because the activity has been so well mastered that it is executed with little or no reflection. Nonetheless, it is true that prior to the mastery of an ability some reflection, perhaps even some deliberation, went into the cultivation of the ability. Even after some skill has been well mastered, it is not simply an unthinking fixed response. Those who have well internalized certain norms of action are able to continue to refine and recreate their technique. The point is that even in routine cases of conduct, there is a sense in which the use of norms still involves a "sense of propriety" or an "interpretation" of some context of conduct. Norms are never completely routine if only because, always being "open" and "alive" in relation to contingent changing circumstances, they are continually being modified through their use in concrete interpretations and judgments.

Conflict

I have already mentioned that norm-governed activities often conflict. The fact that goods are plural, contingent, and particular makes it inevitable that they will conflict. Since goods are the product of norm-governed activity and norms provide possible interpretations of situations, there is the ever-present possibility of conflicting interpretations of goods. Consider two professors who, although committed to education, have deeply divergent interpretations of what a quality education means. They might even agree on some basic claims about what explains the importance of education in the larger life of the community (e.g., it is an integral part of a thriving democracy, etc.) yet still disagree in their specification of this good in the concrete circumstances of their educational practice. Professor A is opposed to the practice of grading students on a "letter system" on the grounds that it tends to lead students to view their education as a means to an external good; it favors conformity, not creativity; it tends to set up a hierarchical system that privileges members of a certain elite class; and so on. Professor B believes the practice of grading on a scale to be integral to maintaining quality standards of excellence. Without these, education will tend to "level out" students to a certain mediocre performance. To some extent the dispute here may hang on the facts about grading—that is, the real consequences either policy would have on student abilities, attitudes, and dispositions. But even though certain facts may be relevant, they are only so relative to a conception of the good of the activity. In some cases the dispute is over this core conception (e.g., Professor A believes education should be based on an apprentice model in which the teacher relates to the student's particular abilities "individually," whereas Professor B believes education requires competition for a necessarily scarce good, namely recognition and honor for academic excellence).

Obviously, this only touches the surface of what an extended debate on this subject would involve. Even though we can grant that understanding the relevance of certain practical considerations in making particular judgments about good involves understanding the point or purpose of the larger enterprise at issue, we should not get the impression that this excludes meaningful honest divergence in interpretations of an enterprise. In many cases (and this may be one) there is no doubt some basic agreement against which the divergent conceptions are argued. Sometimes, disagreement and conflict over the point of an enterprise is a sign of the health and vitality of the enterprise. The question of how much conflict an activity can sustain is a matter that can only be settled empirically.

In conclusion, I want to make clear that I have not defended a complete theory of value in this chapter. I have not attempted to categorize the various kinds of values. Nor have I explored the metaphysical status of values—the "source" of values. My account of value is confined to illustrating the functional role of values in practical justification. The account is therefore "formal" in much the same way that the account of intentional action and practical justification in Chapter 1 was formal. Nevertheless, I believe that a distinctively pragmatist substantive account of value can be given. It seems to me that the pragmatist might claim that "activity" understood as the self-directed expression of a variety of human faculties, including thought, imagination, and emotion, would be a central component of a worked-out value theory.[17] A promising pragmatist-naturalist approach might include explanation of the ways in which genuine human needs are satisfied through expressive activity. Such genuine needs might include the need to express one's identity in a social environment or the need to play and exercise imagination. Such a naturalist account of needs would not violate the pragmatist claim that goods are particular. Like other kinds of general knowledge, knowledge of human needs would not deductively entail conclusions about what action plans to adopt. Rather, such knowledge would serve a useful instrumental purpose in framing action plans, especially with regard to social policies or the creation and reform of institutions. In any case, such an account of value lies beyond the scope of this book.

3 | *Between Universalism and Particularism*

In this chapter I apply the model of norms and values developed in Chapters 1 and 2 to moral principles. I argue that pragmatism provides a compelling, superior middle way between the view that moral judgment is based on universal principles and that of radical particularists who think of moral judgment in terms of case-by-case intuitive responses. In contrast to universalism, pragmatism argues that we ought to reject the notion that moral knowledge must be divided into two domains: knowledge of the justification of principles and knowledge of which principles apply to a specific case. Against radical particularism, pragmatism argues that there is an important place for general moral knowledge in moral judgment.

The model of deliberative events developed in Chapter 1 can be a guide here. Deliberative events about problematic situations make use of general considerations that regulate our efforts to formulate action plans to resolve problems. So the radical particularist idea of responding to particular cases bereft of general knowledge seems like an exaggeration. Yet the view shared by some neo-Kantian universalists that moral judgment is the application of antecedently justified general principles seems inadequate. Such a view passes over the fact that in problem cases principles are not "applied" to arrive at some correct action plan; rather they are used to frame the situation so that we can learn about its salient elements.

Moral problems have a complexity distinct from other kinds

of value problems. This complexity is partly due to the fact that frequently the problem is the way we see our problems. We are sometimes hypocritical, self-deceived, or simply morally blind. In short, it is often hard to determine whether the moral problem lies primarily in aligning an individual's idiosyncratic habits of thinking, feeling, and doing with socially approved moral ways or in the socially approved ways themselves.

This is not to deny that analogous difficulties occur in other nonmoral domains. For example, sometimes it is not clear whether a controversial new artist is simply an amateur—someone who has never adequately assimilated the standards and skills of the relevant artistic traditions. Nevertheless, what might at first look like a failed artist may turn out to be a genius ahead of her time, someone who radically transforms and advances an artistic tradition. What makes the complexity of moral problems distinct is the fact that the norms at stake are integral to a wide range of social relationships. Furthermore, the importance of moral norms shows up in strong evaluations—judgments of praise and blame. People come to apply these strong evaluations to themselves (in conscience) as well as to others. As Dewey puts it:

> In language and imagination we rehearse the responses of others just as we dramatically enact other consequences. We foreknow how others will act, and the foreknowledge is the beginning of judgment passed on action. We know with them; there is conscience. An assembly is formed within our breast which discusses and appraises proposed and performed acts. The community without becomes a forum and tribunal within, a judgment-seat of charges, assessments and exculpations. Our thoughts of our own actions are saturated with the ideas that others entertain about them, ideas which have been expressed not only in explicit instruction but still more effectively in reaction to our acts.[1]

Dewey's remarks about conscience in this passage vividly frame the fact that judgments of praise and blame comprise a large portion of moral life.[2] Conscience and judgments of praise and blame are elements of those habits and norms that we call "moral." In Chapter 4, I defend the hypothesis that those habits or norms that involve responsibilities for relationships comprise the domain of the "moral." The present chapter assumes that we can defend some account of moral domain. My focus in this chapter includes topics such as the nature of moral knowledge, the role of principles in moral deliberation, and the different kinds of moral problems. I believe that the pragmatist view of norms as complex ways of thinking, feeling, and doing provides a superior alternative theory of moral judgment to those offered by universalist principle-based theories and intuitionist particularist theories.

The Case against Universalism and Radical Particularism

JUSTIFICATION AND APPLICATION: A CRITIQUE OF KANTIAN MORAL JUDGMENT

Recall the model of deliberative events from Chapter 1. One important implication of that model is that a correct description of the situation is a vital step in the resolution of a problematic situation. We gain confidence that we have correctly described a situation only after we have formulated, and ultimately acted upon, an action plan. Even action plans that seem to work are always on trial. We may learn later that we did not adequately complete a deliberative event. Or we may learn that some new problem was an inevitable result of the solution to an old one. So our descriptions of a situation change as our perspective changes through time. At the start of a deliberative event, we may have one view of our problem. After the deliberative event has been completed, we may have a quite different view of the "facts."

Many contemporary models of moral judgment take seriously the idea that a careful construal of the particular facts of the case is an important step in the process of moral judgment. Many philosophers hold that "judgment"—the interpretation of the salient particulars of the situation—is an activity *preliminary* to the application of general moral principles. We must construe the "minor premise" in any practical deliberation *before* applying a general moral norm in order to render a particular moral judgment about what action would be right. Moral deliberation begins with the question, What should I (or we) do here in this particular situation? When we raise the question of what sort of action is morally appropriate, it seems that what we do is subsume the case under some more general moral principle. The moral principle is applied to the situation and justifies some action as right. This suggests the simple model of moral deliberation as commencing with a formulation of the "facts of the case" (this action was a lie), which instantiates some general property F (the action type of lying), which is subsumed under some general moral principle P (if any action is one of lying, then that action ought not to be done), yielding the particular moral judgment (I ought not lie).

The pragmatist model of deliberative events questions this division between application and justification. The division is yet another example of the fixed-end view of justificatory structure, applied now to moral judgment. We have general principles that are justified in some special way. These are held fixed antecedently to deliberation. The task of moral judgment is to discern the particulars of the situation so as to determine whether or not a principle applies. The pragmatist response to this model is that at best it represents settled cases where routinized procedures are deployed with relative ease. However, the model does not adequately account for the *learning* that goes on when the situation itself is indeterminate—when established norms fail us. I want to turn now to a closer look at Onora O'Neill's efforts to develop a neo-Kantian model of moral judgment, which, I argue, makes an untenable separation between justification and application.

Recent work in Kantian ethics has shown that it is possible to develop a more nuanced view of moral judgment than that usually attributed to Kant's approach. Kantian ethics is frequently attacked for being overly rigid in its account of absolute rules that block the more nuanced responses needed in the thick of ambiguous and vexing moral problems. Kant's own application of his categorical imperative supports the objection. One need only consider his absolute prohibition against lying, even if doing so will save a life. Nevertheless, with careful attention to everything Kant has to say, neo-Kantians can make a good case for the suggestion that the categorical imperative does not involve, strictly speaking, the application of a principle to concrete situations. Some neo-Kantians claim that there is a place for non-rule-governed judgment at the level of the formulation of the maxims that are tested by the categorical imperative procedure. The idea in rough is that prior to testing maxims of action we must judge the morally salient facts of the case in order to construct the maxim. Such judgment is not itself a matter of applying moral principles or even of using Kant's categorical testing procedure. Principles are indeterminate. They alone cannot tell us what to do. At some point in deliberation we must judge that this case must be subsumed under some principle P.

The argument for the necessity of non-rule-governed judgment is simple. When I am faced with the need to decide whether the principle that says "if any act is one of lying, then that act ought not be done" applies to some action that I am considering, I cannot make this decision by reference to a principle on pain of infinite regress. That is, I must first recognize the action as falling under the appropriate description "lying," and only *then* can I determine that it violates some more general moral principle, thus yielding the particular moral judgment that this action ought not be done.[3] The point here is that the judgment or perception of this case as being one of lying—as falling under that general moral principle—*is not itself* an application of a moral rule. Assume, for a moment, that it is. Then my recognition that an action A is an instance of some general principle P must be decided by reference to some principle P' that indicates that actions of this type fall under P. But then, how do I know that P' applies to this case? On the basis of our initial assumption, this can only be determined by reference to some other principle P'' that indicates that P' applies to those cases in which P applies to A and so on ad infinitum. The point is that we cannot rely on moral rules to escape "judgment." The very claim that we should rely on these rules (as opposed to any of the other myriad rules that might apply to this case) shows that judgment has been made.

O'Neill illustrates this idea of non-rule-determined judgment by way of Kant's notion of "reflective judgment." She says, "The situation of agents is in the first place one that requires reflective judgment: Only when an account or description of a particular case has been given—only when a process of reflection has produced an appraisal of the case—can principles be applied and a solution sought."[4] O'Neill draws on some remarks from Kant's *Critique of Judgment* to show that Kant's moral theory is not unduly rigid. That is, we need not read Kant as believing that his categorical imperative provides us with some sort of algorithmic decision procedure for determining moral obligation. Rather, Kant recognizes that moral principles are of themselves indeterminate with respect to their application in a specific situation. People need to develop a kind of perceptive skill in noticing the relevant features of situations.

Notice that O'Neill claims that *first* a person must "appraise" or "reflectively judge" a situation, and *then* principles can be applied so as to arrive at a solution of what one morally should do. Another way of putting this point is that "without minor premises reasoning cannot be practical,"[5] meaning that we must exercise judgment about the particular situation (minor premise) in order to determine whether some general moral principle (major premise) is applicable in guiding action in some situation. This judgment cannot itself be an application of a rule, for the reasons just given in the regress argument.

For O'Neill, there are two basic phases of practical deliberation: (1) that of appraising or reflectively judging a situation and (2) that of applying principles to the situation described or judged in order to come to some decision about the rightness or wrongness of an action. One of O'Neill's aims is to argue against Wittgensteinian writers who believe that moral reflection should be centered on examining "what we want to say" about various hypothetical examples (usually drawn from literature). She—I think rightly—points out that the Wittgensteinians, by focusing on examples whose moral significance has more or less already been assumed, fail to account for the fact that oftentimes our difficulties lie precisely in determining what sort of case it is that we are dealing with. Is this case one in which the relevant description is that of a person (doctor) killing another (a patient), or is it one in which someone is serving a client's requests in an appropriate way? Is the case one in which a person is lying to a friend or one in which she is helping to build a friend's confidence? In short there are myriad ways one might describe a case, and sometimes there are controversial and conflicting accounts of what sort of classification is appropriate. A good example of such deep conflict can be found in the debate over abortion. Some describe the case as "the murder of a baby"; others describe it as "a woman's decision to abort unwanted fetal tissue."

As has been mentioned, O'Neill points to Kant's Third Critique in order to develop an account of judgment that will do justice to it. Although Kant believes that reflective judgment is not determined by rules, we can adopt what O'Neill calls "strategies of judgment" and what Kant calls some "maxims of reflective judgment" to help guide deliberators in their construal or description of the situation. These are "regulative principles." Kant suggests three: seeking consistency in our judgments, enlarging our thought/attempting to take the standpoint of others, and thinking for oneself.[6]

I have no quarrel with these Kantian regulative principles. Instead I want to examine the claim that ethical deliberators *first* construe a case and *then* bring principles to bear in order to render some decision or particular moral judgment. One way of interpreting this claim is that in any piece of ethical deliberation we need first to determine the facts of the case before applying norms or moral principles. One might be tempted to make this claim partly on the grounds that the semantic content of any moral principle has a descriptive part. A moral principle like "if any action is one of lying, then that action is forbidden" includes within it a descriptive meaning governed by general semantic rules that enable us to refer descriptively to those actions that are lies.

The problem with this last move is that we are not here dealing with the semantics of moral terms but with the psychological processes by which deliberators come to see that a bit of moral discourse applies in a certain way. Appeal to "meaning rules" is of no help here for much the same reason that the application conditions of a rule cannot themselves be applied by rules.

Furthermore, the description of a case already involves the mobilization of moral or normative considerations. That is to say, it is already a *moral* achievement (as opposed to simply a cognitive achievement) for a person to recognize the *moral* salience of the features of a case. O'Neill herself admits that the power of judgment that deliberators develop in order to construe cases is a power of moral judgment. That is to say, we are talking about a *moral* construal (or description) of a case here. But since this construal is guided by moral norms, we need to ask in what sense it is correct to view deliberation as involving two distinct steps: (1) construing the case and (2) applying a moral principle. What would be left for practical reason to do after the case has been construed? After all, if our construal of a case already presupposes that we classify the case as having morally salient features of a certain sort, then haven't we already applied a certain set of moral principles *P1 . . . Pn*? Or if we haven't literally brought them out explicitly as applicable to this case, aren't they at least presupposed in our construal?

The question is, What is left to test after a case has been construed by judgment? That is, once we have formulated a description of the case as "a patient is suffering and requests that life support be ceased," which includes such *moral* considerations as the "rightness of preventing unnecessary suffering" and the "rightness of respecting the autonomy of people by honoring their wishes," one wonders whether there is any further step that involves the application of principles. Perhaps what an O'Neillian Kantian would say is that once we have made out the case by making clear these moral principles, we go on to test these salient moral features of the case by the categorical imperative testing procedure. This suggests that what is actually tested by the categorical imperative are general maxim *types* (e.g., maxims that include the consideration of unnecessary suffering, the making of a promise, and so on). But if this is the case, it would seem that the categorical imperative procedure would be used to test not the specific maxims of a case but rather the *general features* of specific maxims. Furthermore, such testing would presumably already be done prior to any deliberation. That is, we would already know what the general moral considerations are that could be willed universally. The only task for deliberation would be to see what considerations are relevant to just this maxim made out in just this case and *this* would not be decided by the categorical imperative.[7]

We have just seen how this interpretation suggests that the categorical imperative really does no work in testing a particular maxim after the maxim has been made out. But it might be thought (as O'Neill briefly suggests) that the moral principles that could pass the categorical imperative test are employed to help construe the case. We have already granted the primacy of judgment as an activity that, although perhaps guided by principles of both a more regulative sort (such as thinking from a broad-minded perspective) and a more substantive sort (such as tell the truth or do not cause unnecessary suffering), can only subsume particular cases under these general principles via an act of judgment. But granting this already moves our account of ethical judgment beyond the model that says we must *first* construe a case and *then* apply pre-established indeterminate moral principles.

The view that we must reject is that moral judgment involves a mental act that first identifies nonmoral properties and then adds moral predicates to these properties. We should reject the idea that any moral judgment is composed of two separated factors, the nonmoral property that a person might believe to be present in a certain situation and the value predicate that is hitched to the factual property identified in the descriptive predicate.[8]

In my view this "peeling" of the evaluative from the cognitive is distorting. Recognizing a situation as consisting of some set of important facts relevant to a moral judgment requires at least a tacit evaluation that these facts are relevant. Describing the situation as one in which pain occurs is already a description offered by an agent concerned with noticing such features. And this concern reflects a moral ability—an ability to take certain features as salient and worth noticing in the first place. One might regard the pain of another without moral concern. One could simply note that the person is in pain, perhaps giving an account of the physical state that instantiates the pain state. But the fact that we can so regard the pain of another is no objection to the point that I am making here. After all, a criticism of such disregard implies that we notice a failure to take a fact as relevant that ought to be relevant. I do not want to suggest that we are always right about the ways in which we regard the situation. Nor do I deny that through discussion and critical accounting we might be able to improve our responses to and judgments about relevant features of situations. This is just to admit that fallibility.

The fact that our descriptions are guided by evaluative considerations is illuminated by our account of norms as resident in activities and practices. Learning norms involves learning the proper identification and description of a practice or activity. Identifying the kind of situation we are in implies already identifying what sorts of response are appropriate or proper. Conversely, identifying what sort of responses are appropriate or proper involves identifying what kind of situation we are in. As Thomas Green puts it in reference to Will's view that norms are "resident in practices,"

> This fittingness of conduct to setting is often negotiated simply by recognizing what activity it is in which we are engaged. Recognizing the difference between norms of school and home is largely identical with learning what it means to say that this (the place where one is) just *is* the school, the family, or the church. It is pretty much identical with such things as being able to say that we are now not simply tossing the ball, but playing baseball, that we are not now simply stacking stone, but laying a dry-wall.[9]

Again, this does not mean that once we have described what activity we are participating in all moral questions disappear. It does mean that the only place from which we can address moral questions is from "inside" the very practices in which moral and other norms reside. I do not deny that we frequently struggle to abstract ourselves from practices and view them from "outside" because such an external perspective seems necessary to critically evaluate what these practices are all about. For some purposes, it might be useful to go outside our moral practices and describe what they look like from an observer's perspective. But we run the risk of missing the very normative resources necessary for criticism when we engage in such abstraction. I return to the topic of social criticism in Chapter 5.

In Chapter 1, I argued that general rules have an educational function in deliberative events. Moral principles have this *educational function* as well. When good-willed people confront hard cases, they display their commitment to certain justification practices by considering these cases in the light of moral principles. This educational function of principles, together with the theory of norms as ways of thinking, feeling, and doing, offers a view that does justice to the contextual/interpretive nature of moral judgment and the fact that moral judgment seems to involve general knowledge. In the next two sections, I evaluate two kinds of moral particularism: Jonathon Dancy's radical particularism and Albert Jonsen and Stephen Toulmin's new casuistry. Dancy's view is instructive, even if it comes up short in important respects. Jonsen and Toulmin do a better job of demonstrating the role of general knowledge in moral judgment, although their view does suffer some ambiguity that I will evaluate and clarify.

In his article "Ethical Particularism and Morally Relevant Properties,"[10] Dancy arrives at the conclusion that moral reasons are not general principles but rather helpful hints a person might offer to another to get a person to "see the situation" in the same way that he or she does. As Dancy puts it, "The man who provides reasons is not so much providing evidence for his ethical judgment as trying to show his audience how he sees the situation."[11] My argument against Dancy is that this way of viewing the matter fails to account for the important place of giving general reasons to help discover what is best to do in a problematic case. If all reason-giving really amounts to is helping someone to see the case as I do, then we are assuming that at least *I* already have a settled conviction about the case. But we do not always have a settled conviction. Sometimes we need to examine a case carefully together. What we use in such examinations are general considerations, moral principles if you like.

Dancy's view of reason-giving flows from a more basic attack on the existence of general moral principles. Dancy adopts a particularist epistemology of moral judgment. He calls this epistemology "particularist" because he holds that moral judgment first discerns particular wrongs or rights, and only later over time do people generalize to arrive at moral principles. Dancy rejects the claim that moral principles are such empirical generalizations. However, he accepts a particularist epistemology of moral judgment. In this view, moral knowledge is knowledge derived from particular cases (not knowledge of general principles applied to particular cases). Moral knowledge, for Dancy, is *nothing but* knowledge of particular cases. Dancy's basic argument is that if a generalist account of moral knowledge were true, we could not test general principles by examining particular cases (presumably in the way that we can so test theories). This is because "principles are not like theories, for theories explain what is true in particular cases without determining it, while principles determine what is true in particular cases and explain it. So we discover what our particular duties are by relating our general knowledge to the nature of the particular case. In which case it is difficult to suppose that the nature of our particular duties, as revealed by this procedure, could every cause us to reassess the principles from which those particular duties flow."[12] Dancy takes it to be fairly clear that there is something wrong with a view that would simply deny that we can test general principles by particular cases. The point here can be related to claims that I made in Chapter

1 about the limits on practical principles. The particular circumstances of judgment are too complex and too novel ever to expect complete encapsulation in principles. Therefore, it is plausible to expect that experience with particular cases will enable
revision and change in our general moral principles. As far as
this claim goes, I can agree with Dancy. However, it is one thing
to say that we know *both* particulars and generals and quite another thing to claim that we have *no* general moral knowledge
whatsoever. Dancy accepts the latter, whereas my pragmatism
endorses the former. The precise meaning of the claim that we
have both general and particular moral knowledge is complex.
Moral norms are ways of responding to situations. They are generalized patterns resident in activities that involve a sense of
proper procedure. But to say that they are general patterns is
not to say that these patterns are fixed. Their meaning and import is determined by the three-fold context of transmission, interpenetration, and functional interaction discussed in Chapter
1. From the pragmatist view, we should think of principles as
aspects of norms.[13] General principles provide us with general perspectives through which we can regard features of particular situations and activities.

My view is that moral norms are "empirical generalizations"
if we mean very broadly that moral learning occurs through a
process of problem solving. This problem solving involves both
general considerations and particular cases.[14] The general considerations understood to be norms are not fixed but open to
modification in the light of fresh circumstances. Thus linguistic
formulations of a moral norm will not express necessary truths.

In order to demonstrate that it is plausible to view principles
of morality as empirical generalizations I will rebut Dancy's argument that they cannot be. Dancy adopts a particularist epistemology, holding that moral knowledge is derived from particular cases, coupled with a radical ethical particularism that denies
the existence of any general moral principles. His view is that
moral judgments do not generalize to principles but are a kind
of "intuitive induction" in which we "see" that particular acts are

wrong or right. Dancy claims that moral principles do not behave in the same way that ordinary empirical generalizations behave because moral principles have residual effects, whereas ordinary empirical generalizations do not. Consider the following
empirical generalization:

(1)   If x is a tiger, then x has a tail.
(2)   Max is a tiger.
(3)   Assume that Max does not have a tail.

The truth of (2) and (3) certainly does not impugn the truth
of (1)," since (1) is an empirical generalization. This means that
(1) should be stated something like, "Usually, if x is a tiger, then
x has a tail." But Dancy points out that we do not say that Max
somehow has "more of a tail" because he is a tiger.[15] The general truth of (1) does not have any residual effect on Max's status
of lacking a tail. Now consider a so-called moral generalization:

(1)   If y is an act of lying, then y ought not to be done.
(2) A is an act of lying.
(3)   But A ought to be done (because of some other property asso-
       ciated with it, say, the fact that A is also an instance of some
       other moral principle such as "saving lives ought to be done").

Dancy maintains that in this case we want to say that A does
have some lingering property of being wrong or, more precisely,
of being an act that ought not to be done. Although it may be
overall morally right to do A, A does nevertheless have "more of
a wrong" associated with it precisely because it is an act of lying.
This shows the difference between ordinary empirical generalizations and moral principles. Ordinary empirical generalizations
do not have the residual effect that applies to moral principles.

The problem with Dancy's argument comes from his use of
an empirical generalization about an empirical *object* and its properties. It would be more appropriate to consider other kinds of
nonmoral empirical generalizations in order to see whether they
might behave in analogous ways, i.e., that they might display

the residual effect. The obvious sorts of generalizations that we will want to consider are those relating to nonmoral practical reasoning. Consider the following generalizations:

(1)   If you are one run behind in a baseball game with one out and a man on third base, then you ought to try to drive that man in with a sacrifice fly hit.

(2)   If you are going to a large picnic with many young children, then you ought to bring plenty of napkins.

(3)   If you are having chronic sleeping problems, then you ought to take prescription sleeping medication.

Assume that these three practical principles are true in the sense that on the whole, experience has taught us that the procedures or responses advocated in the consequent are good policies to take, given the circumstances mentioned in the antecedent. Of course, such practical principles contain "all things considered clauses." Certain other features of a situation that might defeat the principles, requiring us to not do what is advocated in the consequents. Now, it is quite easy to recognize cases in which these practical principles are defeated but in which there still exists a residual effect very much analogous to the moral case. In (1) we simply have to imagine that the man at bat is a quite lousy hitter generally, and specifically has not gotten a hit off of the particular pitcher in fifteen at-bats. Let's say that the coach gives the sign to "bunt" because this particular hitter seems to have a better chance at not getting an out than if he tried to hit the ball. In this situation, (1) lingers with residual effect in the sense that it is perhaps an overall better thing to not follow the principle here. However, the fact that this batter has to bunt and not drive a man in is indeed a bad feature of the situation. It is bad precisely because we recognize that in some sense (1) applies to situations like this. To see this, consider the fact that before making the call, it would be understandable to allow the hitter to try to get a sacrifice fly or base hit despite factors of the situation that mitigate against this.

In (2) we have only to imagine a situation in which it is simply not practical to bring napkins. Imagine that the picnic is being held at a remote camp site and that the people charged with bringing napkins only remember their charge when they arrive. When they get there, the food is almost done, and all are hungry. Thus, it is not desirable to send someone out to get napkins. By the time they get back, the food will have long been consumed, and those who went to get the item will have missed lunch. So our picnickers rough it out without napkins. The messy children make clear the bad done in violating (2). But overall, it was better not to delay picnic activities for the sake of napkins. Messy children are worth the other good things that come from consuming the picnic lunch now.

Imagine a case of an insomniac who has not slept well in days. However, he has a job interview. He knows that all available over-the-counter sleeping pills will leave him more groggy the next day than if he were simply to stay up the whole night without medication. Therefore, he concludes that it would be better not to take sleeping pills. The overall right thing to do in the situation is to try to get to sleep without pills. Notice that if he is not able to sleep that night, he may justifiably think to himself that there is some bad in the situation—the bad of a torturous night in bed trying to get to sleep. He can see, therefore, the residual effect of (3), while granting that it is better that (3) not be followed in these circumstances because of the desirability of being as mentally sharp as possible the next day.

If these practical principles can count as empirical generalizations from previous instances, then it seems quite clear that an empirical generalization can have the residual effect Dancy claims is not available to it. Dancy's error is to use empirical generalizations about *objects*—empirical concepts of objects—to show that the residual effect does not obtain for such generalizations. But empirical generalizations about appropriate *actions* clearly do display the residual effect. I conclude, then, that we have no reason against the claim that moral principles are empirical generalizations.

JONSEN AND TOULMIN'S "NEW CASUISTRY"

Jonsen and Toulmin's new casuistry merits attention because it presents a compelling example of a kind of particularism that does appear to allow a place for general considerations in moral judgment. They begin their study by citing their own practical experience as a member and an adviser on the National Commission for the Protection of Human Subjects of Biomedical and Behavioral Research from 1975 to 1978. The commission was the result of legislation passed by the United States Congress in response to morally objectionable research undertaken on human subjects such as the experiments on rural black men in Tuskegee, Alabama. Jonsen and Toulmin make the point that members of the commission made the most progress in developing standards when they focused on *particular cases* as opposed to general moral or legal principles. They developed a moral taxonomy, classifying cases based on similar features. It turns out that members agreed more on particular judgments about particular cases than they did about the general principles, theories and reasons they held for these judgments. They write:

> The *locus of certitude* in the commissioner's discussions did not lie in an agreed set of intrinsically convincing *general* rules or principles, as they shared no commitment to any such body of agreed principles. Rather, it lay in a shared perception about what was *specifically* at stake in particular kinds of human situations. Their practical certitude about specific kinds of cases lent to the commission's collective recommendations a kind of conviction that could never have been derived from the supposed theoretical certainty of the principles which individual commissioners appealed to in their personal accounts. In theory their particular concrete moral judgments should have been strengthened by being "validly deduced" from universal abstract ethical principles. In practice the general truth and relevance of those universal principles turned out to be less certain than the soundness of the particular judgments for which they supposedly provided a "deductive foundation."[16]

This experience led Jonsen and Toulmin to explore the suppressed tradition of casuistry. *The Abuse of Casuistry* attempts to trace the historical development of "case-based" moral reasoning and to develop a positive theoretical proposal for the proper way of thinking about moral argument. In what follows, I shall be concerned mainly with their own positive proposals.

John D. Arras points out in his critical article "The Revival of Casuistry in Bioethics"[17] that Jonsen and Toulmin invert the standard way of thinking about the relation between particular moral judgments and general principles and theories. Instead of attempting to work out some general moral theory that explains and articulates a moral principle or set of principles from which we can deduce necessary conclusions about morally justified actions, they advocate a "bottom-up" approach. We should begin our deliberations by focusing on the particular circumstances surrounding a moral problem. As we decide on particular cases, we gradually build up a moral taxonomy of "paradigm cases." We start with simple agreed-upon cases, such as "Return borrowed goods." We then move out to harder cases, such as "You should not return a borrowed weapon to a person who in a fit of anger demands it."

Two perilous roads may tempt advocates of the "bottom-up" approach to moral theory. One is the radically particularist view, which holds that principles are simply *summaries of the results* of particular judgments about particular cases. In this view, every moral decision is unique, and no general principles can be used to guide deliberation. This seems to be Dancy's view. Since radical particularism is flawed, it is fortunate that a plausible rendering of Jonsen and Toulmin's view is not committed to it. For one thing, in their historical discussion of Greek morality, they view Aristotle's ethics as a *middle road* between the radical particularism of the sophists and Plato's attempt to formulate a moral geometry.[18] Secondly, the emphasis on developing a moral *taxonomy* of type cases suggests that we *can* formulate general procedures that can help guide future deliberations. These types of cases are not "fixed rules" of conduct, but they do furnish us with general considerations that help to orient and organize our moral reflection about particular problems. Case types are empirical generalizations generated from particular encounters with past problem-solving events, which can be thought of as representations of deliberative events that include both detailed action plans and the problematic situations to which these plans are responses.

Nevertheless, this talk of "moral taxonomy," "cases," and "paradigms" can lead us down another path that I believe ultimately undermines what is most promising in Jonsen and Toulmin's work. The development of a moral taxonomy might suggest the project of formulating ever more elaborate and detailed moral principles. The more information we pack into our principles, the better prepared we are to cope with practical life. This view would aim at a kind of moral rule book. Our book of rules might never be fully complete, but we could still aspire to such completeness by careful and meticulous cataloging of cases. If this path is taken, the resulting moral rules would consist of universal principles. The priority of particular cases, in this account, would be a *priority of detailed moral principles.*

I do not believe Jonsen and Toulmin endorse this view any more than the radically particularist view.[19] Nevertheless, their talk of moral taxonomies and cases lends itself to this sort of interpretation. Matters are further complicated when they occasionally mishandle the notion of "universality"—seemingly rejecting it as a feature of moral considerations. As R. M. Hare points out, one can develop *elaborate, detailed* principles that can be universalized as long as they pick out "properties."[20] For example, the following principle is perfectly universal in form: "If you are a doctor who has diagnosed a patient with meningitis and the results show that it is 90 percent likely it is not fatal, you should advise the patient of the 10 percent chance that could be fatal kind. You should then recommend staying in the hospital for observation overnight." The principle might be further detailed: "If your patient understands the risks and still requests to be let go . . ." and so on. The point is that no matter how "detailed" a principle may be, it can still be universalized. Principles can be universalized whether they be a simple code of conduct like "Don't steal" or an elaborate specification of the conditions under which one should not steal. Simply put, one should not equate *generality* (or *abstractness*) with *universality*.

The correct response a casuist *should* make to Hare's point is not to deny that elaborate detailed cases cannot be universalized. The casuist instead ought to argue that the focus on cases *should not* be confused with focus on elaborate rules. The priority of the particular, in the casuist account, should be taken to mean the priority of *interpreting* the particular problematic case. Our aim, in many kinds of moral problems, is to formulate an action plan that gives a correct response and a correct interpretation of the situation that we are in.

Statements like the following suggest that Jonsen and Toulmin are not completely clear about whether they erroneously deny universalizability of rules because rules can be so complicated, or they accept Hare's point and go on to argue that it is not so much mistaken as beside the more important point that we must always keep an interpretive eye open for relevantly *dissimilar* features of the case now before our judgment. After reviewing the history of casuistry, they offer up their own definition of casuistry as "the analysis of moral issues, using procedures of reasoning based on paradigms and analogies, leading to the formulation of expert opinions about the existence and stringency of particular moral obligations, framed in terms of rules or maxims that are general but not universal or invariable, since they hold good with certainty only in typical conditions of the agent and circumstances of action."[21] In this passage it appears that "universal" is conflated with "invariable" and contrasted with "general." But obviously, if a paradigm or case is framed in terms of "typical" conditions, the resulting statement or principle describing the paradigm is perfectly well universalizable. One could say, "In such and such circumstances this act is appropriate," adding, "as long as conditions are 'normal' and there are no 'rebutting' factors."

Nevertheless, shortly after giving this definition of casuistry, Jonsen and Toulmin offer a more cautious statement. In a discussion of "high casuistry" they write,

As always in practical reasoning, casuistry *offered limited scope for universal,* invariable generalizations. If "high casuists" hesitated to universalize their judgments, or to say "never" when it was more correct to say "well, hardly ever" or "never in any circumstances we have yet considered," they were acting like Supreme Court justices who eschew obiter dicta and refuse to present opinions going beyond the facts of the immediate cases, for fear that they may prejudice ("prejudge") issues that may yet arise in some future case, the detailed facts of which are not yet available for their consideration.[22]

This passage presents a clearer view of why it is problematic to think of the results of practical reasoning about moral problems in "universal" terms, namely, that practical life is so complex that we must always be ready to revise and change our considered judgments in light of new experience. A more plausible rendering of Jonsen and Toulmin's position is not the denial of the universal form of statements about paradigms or cases that result from practical deliberation but rather as offering the following cautionary advice: "Do not get fixated on rules and principles (even of the detailed sort). Doing so will tend to take you away from being open to relevant facts that may crop up in future circumstances. To be sure, we can and do settle on adequate procedures for action. We have some central cases whose violation is beyond the pale (e.g., killing or torturing the innocent for pleasure). But we cannot expect that the cases we have found agreement on will be adequate or relevant to all future circumstances."

My first reservation about Jonsen and Toulmin's "case-based" account of moral reasoning is that we can easily be misguided down two undesirable paths. I do not deny that a detailed moral taxonomy or classification of cases can be useful. Such classifications are best viewed as tools for helping to resolve new problems. Furthermore, such paradigms can themselves be viewed as perfectly universalizable principles. The real issue, then, is not whether we are for or against universalization in ethics. It is, rather, how we are to understand the use of moral norms and what it is appropriate to focus on in moral deliberation and argument.

THE CONNECTION BETWEEN PRACTICAL JUDGMENT
AND THEORETICAL KNOWLEDGE

I have just voiced some reservations or dangers in talk of "cases." My suggestion is to keep clear that claims about the "priority of the particular" are claims about the centrality of "case *construing*." Recall Jonsen and Toulmin's claim that the locus of moral certitude is centered on particular judgments (not the general principles that might be thought to account for them). Even if we set aside interpreting this claim to be radically particularist, one might still wonder how the view escapes being categorized as some sort of intuitionism—perhaps one in which we "see" only that particular acts are right or wrong. It is clear that the kind of "perception" or "particular judgment" that Jonsen and Toulmin have in mind here is the *recognition of patterns*—of particular *kinds* of circumstances—not mysterious intuitions of unique particulars. Practical knowledge is concerned with specific problems. In this respect, Jonsen and Toulmin maintain that we can draw an analytic contrast between theoretical science and practical knowledge. First, scientists tend to be concerned with particular examples only insofar as they illustrate some general theoretical principle. In contrast, individuals in practical fields such as law and medicine use general ideas *indirectly*. They are immersed in the particulars of certain clients with unique needs and interests. Secondly, scientists seek after claims that have theoretical necessity inasmuch as they seek to discover laws of nature. Practitioners, on the other hand, are primarily concerned with treating specific, perhaps unique, problems. A lawyer does employ general knowledge of law (as well as other relevant bodies of knowledge) in order to make the best possible case for a particular client. But the use of this general knowledge is subservient to the needs of a particular case. A doctor draws on the results of biological science. But this knowledge is subservient to the immediate task of determining what is appropriate to cure this particular patient with these particular symptoms.

Consider the relation between biological theory and clinical judgment. Jonsen and Toulmin point out that on the one hand, clinical judgment has always required an element of skill in practical judgment. The doctor must observe the set of symptoms exemplified by the patient and then by analogical reasoning, attempt to match these symptoms to other cases in order to see what sorts of medical procedures might be appropriate. On this level of clinical diagnosis, a doctor need not grasp the underlying biological principles.

On the other hand, it should be obvious that biological science is an immensely useful tool for the practice of clinical medicine. However, it would be a mistake to think that biological theory provides the "axioms" from which (by way of formal entailment relations) one could deduce clinical judgments:

> Biology does not bear on clinical medicine in any simple or direct (let alone formal) way: their interrelations are substantial and subtle. . . . On the one hand, the rights and wrongs of any clinical procedure, as a way of treating a particular patient's current condition, is never simply or formally "deducible from" the general principle or biological theory: no strict deductive links hold between them. Where the mechanisms of the disease that a particular patient presents are scientifically understood, the practitioner can properly draw on that understanding as intellectual background to his clinical decisions. But clinical knowledge does not automatically give out at the point where biology runs out of steam. If a case does not fall clearly within one or another of the classes of disease of which we have a full scientific grasp, the clinical tasks of diagnosis and treatment are less open to theoretical understanding, but they are no less typical elements of clinical practice. . . . On the other hand, just because the general biomedical theories and particular clinical decisions are not linked by a medical "geometry," there is no reason to despair of the substantive "rights" and "wrongs" of clinical decisions. Even without a rigorous theoretical basis, clinical judgments are not (as some would argue) the personal hunches or expressions of taste within which individual doctors respond to each practical situation in turn. The guarantees of medical objectivity do not, in practice, depend only on formal theoretical entailments: the strongest support for agreeing to a clinical diagnoses of a therapeutic proposal comes from substantive medical evidence.[23]

A medical argument recommending a certain procedure for curing a disease is to be viewed as a case made within a larger norm-governed context that does involve bodies of medical knowledge. This knowledge bears subtle "substantive" connections to particular clinical judgments. Theoretical conceptions are used with an eye to their usefulness in solving particular problems. Instead of thinking of moral theories as sets of principles from which one can deduce necessary particular judgments, we should think of general moral conceptions as useful aids for illuminating practical problems. Pragmatists think of theories in the philosophical tradition not as mutually exclusive accounts of the correct truth about morality but rather as partially correct tools to be used to understand and resolve particular kinds of problems.

Pragmatist Theory of Moral Principles

The neo-Kantian, radical particularist, and casuist theories of moral judgment offer us three distinct notions of generality in ethics: (1) The neo-Kantian holds that *indeterminate general moral principles* are necessary for constructing particular moral judgments. (2) The radical particularist maintains that general moral considerations are *response patterns* that may be gleaned after particular judgments are made. (3) The casuist holds that generality is centered on *type cases* that may involve detailed descriptions of circumstances. Casuists suggest, further, that general theoretical conceptions are important only as long as they are understood as subservient to solving a particular problem.

These three accounts offer *partial* truths that can be gathered into a more comprehensive and adequate view. O'Neill's Kantianism involves an untenable division between justification of principles and application of principles: however, she hints at a promising theory of moral principles as indeterminate regulative strategies. Dancy's brand of radical particularism rests on an untenable argument against knowledge of general moral principles, and it falsely denies the range of problem cases in which people use moral principles to learn together about what should be done. Yet it does point in the direction of the fundamental insight that moral norms, like other practical considerations, are patterned ways of thinking, feeling, and doing. Jonsen and Toulmin's casuistry is promising in its focus on paradigm cases as the locus of moral knowledge, as long as we do not fall into ambiguity about what is meant by a "case."

When we take the pragmatist view of norms as concrete ways of feeling, thinking, and doing, and we adopt the view that deliberative events are ways of mediating norms that have become problematic, then we can make better sense of these three types of generality. These types of generality should be classified in terms of their function in norm-governed conduct. I now explore these functions in more detail.

ROUTINE MORAL JUDGMENT

The first type of generality is the notion that moral norms involve response patterns that we might identify after enough observation. Pragmatism claims that norms or habits are *ways* of thinking, feeling, and doing. People who have acquired moral habits or norms are in many ways like people who have acquired expertise in nonmoral skills like swimming. An ability such as swimming is a complex pattern that is realized on different occasions in different ways. Realizing an ability in different circumstances is not a matter of having a rule or concept in one's mind and using it to guide behavior through the situation. The expert swimmer usually does what is appropriate in the right circumstances. The same is true of a person who has acquired some moral norm like truth-telling. The moral person can be *counted* on to act in certain ways in a routine situation.[24] The morally good person sees, feels, and thinks about her world in certain reliable ways. The truthful person can be counted on to tell the truth, and she does so reliably with little or no hesitation or deliberation. This does not mean, as Dewey points out, that she expresses truthfulness in some specific rote way. Her habit of truthfulness may show up subtly in a certain open or candid letter-writing style as easily as it might show up in more vivid ways, such as admitting moral wrong-doing to a friend.[25]

The kinds of behavior or actions that count as expressions of the truth-telling norm depend on the background context. Truth-telling in a family or friendship differs from truth-telling in the workplace. This is so, in part, because of the other norms and other particular circumstances that govern these differing activities. We do not follow single norms but clusters of interpenetrating norms.[26]

Now, just as we have beginning swimmers, we also have moral novices. Young children need to learn what the rule of truth-telling means, and they need to acquire the ways of acting and feeling that are appropriate to this moral norm. This takes time and training on intellectual and emotional levels. Children are moral novices in the sense that they have moral potentials. We may speak of other moral "novices" who fail to reliably respond to routine situations, perhaps because they are crazy, uninformed, or evil. I will group these cases of moral failure under the label "decision problems." The common feature of decision problems is that these involve failures in the development and/or expression of moral habits. Here are examples of such as decision problems:

(P1) Some "passions"—what we referred to in Chapter 1 as disorganized systems of habits—interfere with the acquisition or expression of a moral norm.

(P2) A person may be incompetent, and thus incapable of moral reasoning and moral behavior.

(P3) A person may lack the appropriate factual knowledge, and thus make a faulty assessment of the what moral norms are relevant.

(P4) A person may simply disregard morality, as in cases of so-called moral evil.

(P5) The person may not yet have acquired full moral agency. The paradigmatic case is a young child.

DETERMINATION PROBLEMS

Decision problems are primarily problems with the habits of a particular individual, involving a failure to acquire moral norms.

Determination problems are failures in the socially shared norms themselves. In a determination problem, we use O'Neill's second type of generality: indeterminate regulative principles.

Dewey makes a distinction between what he calls "rules" and "principles" that is illustrative of the difference between determination and decision problems. Consider the following passage:

> *Rules are practical; they are habitual ways of doing things. But principles are intellectual; they are the final methods used in judging concrete courses of action. . . . [T]he object of moral principles is to supply standpoints and methods which will enable the individual to make for himself an analysis of the elements of good and evil in the particular situation. . . .* A moral principle . . . gives the agent a basis for looking at and examining a particular question that comes up. It holds before him certain possible aspects of the act; it warns him against taking a short or partial view of the act.[27]

Moral principles regulate particular moral judgments in those cases in which no clear norm furnishes us with an adequate response. They help us construe salient features of determination problems. A moral rule, on the other hand, can be taken as a routine norm or habit in the sense of a patterned response to certain typical situations. When circumstances are such that these established ways of acting fail to guide conduct, we must reflect on the situation and the morally salient features in order to "construe" and devise some solution.

We might ask whether this view of moral principles as "strategies of judgment" really amounts to W. D. Ross's prima facie position.[28] If we build on the model of norms set out in Chapter 1, we can see why the prima facie theory is not an adequate alternative. Pragmatist practical reasoning centers on deliberative events that include possible action plans as solutions to problematic situations. People construct deliberative events when they are struggling to see what they ought to do. Moral problems, like other practical problems, involve the use of general considerations, or principles. James D. Wallace makes this point in the following passage:

If all I know about truth-telling as a practical consideration is that we have a reason to tell the truth, I do not understand about truth-telling. The sort of practical knowledge that moral agents have when they know about truth-telling as a moral consideration, when they understand the principle that they should tell the truth, consists in a great deal more than just the knowledge that they have reason to tell the truth. One has a fuller or lesser knowledge and understanding of truth-telling as a practical consideration depending on the extent of one's understanding of the importance of truth in various areas of life, why it is important, and how it is to be compared in importance with other considerations that pertain in these areas. A corollary of this last claim is that one cannot understand a consideration such as truthfulness in isolation.[29]

Wallace's point here is important to keep in mind when we make the claim that moral principles regulate judgment about problem cases. O'Neill's use of Kantian "maxims of reflection" or "regulative principles" is helpful. These principles are generalized "strategies," which do not prescribe specific actions but rather lead us toward a broader "intersubjective" point of view from which to consider actions. When we view all moral principles in this way, we must resist the claim that these thin, indeterminate principles are *themselves* justificatory reasons to do what is mentioned in their content. The point here is an application of the argument made in Chapter 1: in problematic cases, general practical considerations function as a stage in a deliberative event aiming at forming an action plan that will adequately mediate conflicting but interpenetrating habits.[30]

We should not get the impression from the analytic distinction between determination and decision problems that these types of problems are always neatly separable. Sometimes we need to change primarily the practitioners so that their habits express established norms. Sometimes we need to alter the norms. Oftentimes, however, it is not clear whether the problem is in the person or the norm. Is the disruptive behavior of a group of students in an elementary school to be dealt with by direct punitive measures? Or are the existing punitive measures themselves either a contributor to, or useless for, the prevention of the disruptive behavior? Is the problem mainly that of reforming an individual's motivational structure (getting him to overcome some decision problem) or is it that of changing the norms of the institution (solving a determination problem)? These matters cannot be settled in abstraction from detailed attention to the concrete problem. What we can see in general, however, is that determination and decision problems lie on a continuum.

So-called ideological distortions present examples of how intertwined determination and decision problems may become. Presumably in these sorts of problems there is an interplay between moral pathologies in individuals and failures in the norms governing basic social institutions. At one time the demand for a more or less unconditional property right might have been reasonable (e.g., when individuals were attempting to break free of the yoke of feudal arrangements). But as the use of such property rights becomes conjoined with economic arrangements that force masses of people to sell wage labor to those few who own the means of production, this right becomes problematic. However, the problematic nature of this right is obfuscated by the interest that a dominant class has in maintaining power (partly behind the cover of legitimation by fundamental rights). Ideological distortion is on the one hand clearly "internal" to individuals—an inability to see a social order for what it is. On the other hand, the means for surmounting this kind of problem are deeply connected to certain systematic institutional and social forces.

The Anatomy of Moral Argument

We have just explored two related senses of generality in moral norms. The first is in norms as routine ways of thinking, feeling, and doing. The second is norms as general intellectual instruments for framing problematic cases. These two types of generality reflect two kinds of *norm use*. The third type of generality— expressed by the casuist idea of detailed type cases—can be captured by our model of a deliberative event. Representations of deliberative events may mention particular detailed case facts, salient general moral considerations, and the action plans proposed as resolutions. These complex representations might themselves be taken as regulative principles when they are carried over from one problem to another.

Moral argument about determination problems is an attempt to construct a deliberative event that could command assent. The representation of a deliberative event is essentially what Jonsen and Toulmin call "cases" or "paradigms." Recall that in their experience more progress was made in constructing moral standards for human subjects when cases, not general principles, were the focus of discussion and debate. The pragmatist could argue that it is more productive to view moral arguments as efforts to complete deliberative events with action plans that could win wide assent in a community. When people in a debate over abortion, for example, focus on general principles such as "It is wrong to take a life" or "A woman has a right to control her own body," a number of obstacles are likely to crop up. First, general moral platitudes admit many possible interpretations. Everyone agrees in the abstract that killing innocent life is wrong. The question is whether this principle is relevant in the case of abortion. The second point is that focus on general principles frequently takes people away from careful and intelligent inspection of particular facts of the problem. Third, a focus on general principles tends to foster an attitude of moral righteousness. Defenders of "life" tend to take themselves to be the morally upright who must fight against evil people who kill innocent babies, whereas defenders of "choice" may in turn vilify people who are pro-life as completely insensitive to woman's issues. In short, if we are too quick to frame moral disagreement in terms of general moral principles, we are apt to be too quick to frame the moral problem as a decision problem—as a problem with those who are either too stupid, selfish, or evil to see their own moral sins.

In light of these kinds of considerations, the remainder of this chapter will be devoted to developing the main features of what I consider to be an account of the ingredients of good moral argument. My claim is that the third sense of generality—the generality of a deliberative event and its action plan—represents part of our conception of good moral deliberation, especially with regard to moral argument and debate about difficult determination problems. Practicing this kind of moral argument does not necessarily lead to easy or clean results. I contend that it does, however, avoid some of the difficulty.

In what follows I will first lay out a model of practical argument that Toulmin first presented in his book *The Uses of Argument*.[31] I reply to the charge that "case-based" models of moral argument fall prey to being too narrowly focused on particular problems at the expense of "larger" questions regarding socially accepted values.

TOULMIN'S ACCOUNT OF PRACTICAL ARGUMENT

When we are called on to provide justifications for action plans, we typically refer to certain "data" or "facts of the case," which we take to ground some conclusion. Some simple examples will show this. "Why did you leave work early today?" "Because my child was ill and needed to be picked up from day care." "Why do you think that it is best to give him a dose of methadone?" "Because he requested it for the pain in his leg." Of course these bare statements do not tell us much. This is because usually the context in which grounds are provided is implicitly understood by all concerned. There are many occasions in which we need go no further than to cite the facts of the case as grounds for some justifiable action. There are many other cases in which some procedure is so routine that explicit appeal to grounds is unnecessary. Toulmin offers the following representation of such practical arguments:

$$D \rightarrow \text{so } C$$

The connection between D (the data) and C (the conclusion) requires a bridging principle—a rule of inference that licenses the inference from certain facts of the case to a conclusion about appropriate action. Toulmin points out that typically this rule is simply implicitly assumed. He calls such rules "warrants." If called on we could spell out exactly *why* it is we are entitled to our conclusion on the basis of these "facts of the case": "Since it is permissible to leave work early for a family emergency, and my child was ill at day care, I decided to clock out of work an hour early that day." "Since doctors should do all they can to alleviate the pain of their patients and this patient was in great pain, I concluded that it would be best to administer the methadone." We can now represent the practical argument thus:

(D)   My child became ill at day-care → so *(C)* it was permissible to leave work early to pick him up

|

because

|

(W)   it is permissible to leave work early in order to attend to a family emergency.

Such practical arguments do not guarantee that their conclusions follow "necessarily" from their premises. The strength of the conclusion is a matter of greater or lesser strength depending on the weight of the grounds and warrant offered. And the weightiness of such grounds can only be determined by looking at the details of the case. We can speak of the "force" of the conclusion of an argument (e.g., likely, probable, most certain, necessary, and so forth). Toulmin refers to the force of the conclusion as the "modal qualifier." Related to this point are what we might call "rebutting circumstances," which are those conditions under which we would have to set the warrant aside, thereby prohibiting the move from the data to conclusion. With these points in mind we can now fill out our example as follows:

(D)   My child became ill at day care → so *(Q)* (probably) it was permissible to leave work early to pick him up

|

unless *(R)* (. . . .)

|

(W)   it is permissible to leave work early in order to attend to a family emergency.

Toulmin rightly reminds us that it is important to keep these components of practical arguments clear and separate. The extent to which we focus on these component parts of a practical argument will vary depending on the circumstances. Sometimes the problem is merely that of whether D holds true. Was he really sick? Did the man's behavior indicate that he was experiencing extreme physical pain, or was he just in a bad mood? Sometimes the dispute is over the force of the conclusion in light of rebutting circumstances: "Sure, typically a sick child would be grounds for letting you off work early. However, you could have stayed fifteen minutes longer, couldn't you? Given the importance of finishing this project and getting it in the mail today, it seems under these circumstances you shouldn't have left early."

So far, we might think of the model presented as representative of moral reasoning in its *routine phase.* Such reasoning is not concerned with the resolution of determination problems. It is tedious to point out the fact that understanding the above argument requires that one understand what it is to be a parent, the meaning of illness, and so forth. But recognition of this larger interpretive frame becomes vital when the warrants cited in practical argument themselves become problematic.

Sometimes warrants themselves are thrown into question and require what Toulmin calls a "backing." In the above case the backing for the warrant might be as follows:

(B)   On account of the fact that obligations to family members in an emergency typically override other obligations, it seems reasonable to conclude that one is permitted to leave work early in order to tend to a sick child.

In some cases we might think of the warrant-establishing "backing" as itself another more general warrant. But it is better not to confuse the level of warrant-establishing arguments with the level of warrant-using arguments. Typically, when we are concerned with establishing a warrant, it is because there is some reasonable doubt about its adequacy in a given case. Perhaps another warrant is thought to cover the case with equal force.

We need to consider the two warrants to see which "backing" is stronger. Perhaps a new warrant is being put forth to resolve a novel problem. Rational acceptance of the new warrant requires a plausible justificatory rationale; that is, it requires the spelling out of the backing that establishes the said warrant.

Recall the model of a deliberative event from Chapter 1:

(1)   There is an indeterminate situation, including a felt sense of trouble due to a failure of habits.

(2)   There is a preliminary interpretation of the problem, including a view of what important goods and evils are at issue.

(3)   Action plans are created that attempt to take account of the important goods and evils at issue.

(4)   These action plans are tested in imaginative trials.

(5)   The most promising plan is tested in actions bringing about change in the situation.

(6)   1–5 can be repeated by others or used to explain to others what was learned.

We can think of steps 3 and 4 as conclusions of warrant-establishing arguments designed to formulate action plans. After we have settled our debates, the time for action arrives. We act with a careful eye to consequences. If the problem appears to be resolved, then the representation of the entire deliberative event in steps 1–5 can be used to guide further deliberations and arguments in the future (through the explanation mentioned in step 6). Nevertheless, the pragmatist position is fundamentally fallibilist. We must be willing to admit that deliberative events that we thought were closed might actually remain open. We must also be prepared for the fact that resolutions of one deliberative event may lead to new problems requiring new deliberations.

THE MORAL BLINDER OBJECTION

Warrant-establishing arguments require that we make explicit certain salient latent features of some norm-governed context of activity. It is in the context of such warrant-establishing arguments that we often debate certain "large" or "deep" normative questions—questions about the nature of moral personality, our most fundamental ideals, and the kind of moral community that we want to be. These "large" considerations are often left presupposed, but they nevertheless exert an influence on the ways in which we interpret our moral world. We might say that they constitute the sediment of "moral common sense."

Consider now the moral blinder objection to Jonsen and Toulmin's case-based account of moral reasoning. Arras holds that by focusing on particular cases—particular problems of people in particular activities or professions—we may tend to limit our "moral vision." In short, we will be blinded from examination of the big value questions. By focusing on particular moral cases we might lose sight of larger questions about "fundamental values." As Arras puts it, "The kind of reasoning by analogy championed by the new casuists tends to reduce our field of ethical vision down to the proximate moral precedents and thereby suppresses the important global questions bearing on who we are and what kind of society we want. The result is likely to be a method of moral reasoning that graciously accommodates any and all technological innovations, no matter what their potential long-term threat to fundamental and cherished institutions and values."[32] It is understandable how talk of "cases" can suggest a kind of narrow concern with a particular quandary in some narrow field of activity. This is part of the reason that we must not forget that focus on cases is a focus on *case interpretation.* The ways in which we think of cases and the uses that they may serve can vary depending on the context, concerns, and interests of agents. These might concerns may in fact be "large" value questions. An example will help. Veatch refers to the case of Beth Williams, a woman who worked as a file clerk with limited income and obligations as a single parent. She became ill with an ear infection and consulted a doctor who advised that she purchase a prescription of an expensive antibiotic to reduce the risk of failure. Presumably, this recommendation was based on the doctor's knowledge that the cheaper generic drugs tend not to be as effective as the more expensive brands. Nonetheless, Williams wanted the cheapest brand possible. However, the doctor insisted that one should not take chances with ear infections. Veatch nicely states some of the underlying conflicts in this case:

> Buried among the technical, pharmacological judgments made by the physician about the relative safety and efficacy of the trade name and generic name products are a number of value judgments. Since the situations of the physician and her patient differ, it is reasonable to suspect that their values may differ as well. Possibly because of her income level, the physician is unimpressed by her patient's request for the cheapest product. For her, the admittedly small degree of extra confidence in the trade name product is worth the extra cost. Mrs. Williams, earning only $6200 as a file clerk, probably places a very different value on the $8.50.[33]

The example may be used to illustrate issues that transcend the conflict between a particular doctor and her patient. It shows the different sorts of interpretive value horizons that are at play in assessing the worth of certain medical options. The divergence in value judgment in this case can be explained (at least partly) by the differing socioeconomic positions of patient and doctor. Think of the different sorts of moral and political reflection that this kind of example may provoke. One may use cases like this to get doctors to critically reflect on how the economic status of a patient might bear on concrete medical choices. Examples such as this might also help us to reflect on large policy questions about how appropriate it is to distribute (at least a large share of) medical goods according to market principles and mechanisms.

It seems, then, that once we recognize how the ways in which we arrive at particular judgments depend on features of the norm-governed contexts that set the stage for particular problems, we should have no worry that somehow focusing on cases will lead to a narrowing of our ethical vision. The model that I have been working with shows how we can telescope moral problems in two directions. On the one hand we can (and many times must) focus on the need to come to a decision about very particular problems in very particular circumstances. This focus is structured by a rich set of normative background considerations. On the other hand, we can look through the other end of the telescope at the larger normative context that sets the stage for particular judgments. When our warrants fall into disarray, we often have occasion for such reflection. But sometimes we can and should reflect on these larger features so that we have some sense of direction prior to dealing with actual, sometimes painfully difficult, moral problems.

INTERPRETIVE CONFLICT: AN EXAMPLE

But now, a second objection may be raised. How do we resolve disagreements about warrants when these disagreements are based in divergent interpretive horizons—divergent ideals and "fundamental" values—different "backings"? Veatch describes the case of a skier named Morrow who suffered a leg injury. He was brought into the hospital with a compound fracture of the femur. Morrow's leg was set by Dr. Olson, who subsequently prescribed a "propoxyphene compound," which consisted of aspirin and a nonnarcotic chemical. This chemical is nonaddictive but also lacked the painkilling potency of a narcotic. As Morrow recovered from the anesthesia, he experienced great pain, requesting some form of relief. The nurse on duty gave him another dose of propoxyphene, but this did not sufficiently blunt the pain. On the verge of screaming from agony, Morrow requested a stronger painkiller. The nurse asked Dr. Barnett—the resident on call—to come and prescribe another medication. Barnett prescribed a narcotic. The next morning, upon hearing of the prescription, Dr. Olson scolded Dr. Barnett: "Who says the physician's job is to use every technical trick just to make the patient happy? I took an oath pledging that I would do what would benefit my patient, not what would turn him on for the moment. The body is something very delicate, something sacred. . . . Tamper with the body as little as you can."[34] Dr. Barnett justifies his choice according to the view that the tools of modern medical science should be used to intervene in bodily process to alleviate unnecessary pain whenever possible.

We could characterize the clash between these two doctors as a clash between two warrants:

> *W1:* In those circumstances in which a patient is suffering pain and requests medication to relieve the pain, one ought only resort to narcotics as a "last resort" (i.e., in extreme situations).
>
> *W2:* In those circumstances in which a patient is suffering pain and requests medication to relieve the pain, one may prescribe whatever medications are sufficient to relieve the pain (taking precautions to prevent bodily harm or drug addiction).

Obviously in this case, nobody disputes the "fact" that Morrow is in pain. What is in dispute is the *relevance* of this fact to possible medical responses. Both warrants only yield "presumptive" conclusions. That is, both warrants allow for rebutting circumstances. In effect, when Olson and Barnett offer their rationales in the above example, they are attempting to establish their respective warrants. They are appealing to differing "backings" for these warrants. Veatch rightly points out that the differing rationales that these doctors appeal to are based on divergent background value considerations. In fact, they are based on much larger "theories" or "philosophies" of human health and well-being, as well as views on the proper scope and limits of using human technology to intervene in "natural processes." Dr. Olson's view is based on the concept of "homeostasis," "the notion that the body has a natural tendency to maintain a relatively stable state."[35] Veatch points out that this "medical" theory, formulated by Walter Cannon, is imbued with values. It expresses a certain normative conception of the appropriate relation of human beings to natural processes. This conception results in the view that the body possesses a kind of internal "wisdom," "which should be tampered with only with fear and trembling."[36] Another conception behind Olson's judgment in this case might be a concern with possible effects of drug addiction, which would result in more harm than any short-term benefits of alleviating the pain.

Dr. Barnett, on the other hand, arrives at his judgment from a different set of background value conceptions. He appears to hold to the view that "man . . . shall have dominion over the

earth and subdue it. Technological man of the modern West is
man the maker. . . . This philosophy of the rational organization
to solve the problems of the world has produced the great medical miracles. Average life-expectancy has doubled. Suffering has
been relieved. What was once thought to be the inevitable force
of an evil spirit is now swept away with the mere injection of
penicillin."[37] Furthermore, Dr. Barnett may have a different assessment of the likelihood of long-term addiction. Or he may
simply "put more value" on the immediate need to relieve the
extreme suffering of the patient.

We ought to avoid two extreme views of the "value conflicts"
presented by the example. On the one hand, we should not exaggerate the amount of conflict and incommensurability at stake.
We may assume that Barnett and Olson agree, for example, that
certain other sorts of extraordinarily strong narcotics should not
be used, that any narcotic if used needs to be closely monitored,
and so forth. Furthermore, we may assume that at least some of
the dispute can in principle be settled by more factual inquiry. It
may be that one of the judgments of the likelihood of addiction
can be shown to be wrong (or at lease not as likely) on the basis
of empirical studies. Nevertheless, we should not, on the other
hand, assume that "the facts" will necessarily settle the dispute.
After all, we might assume that both doctors are equally informed
on the best theories of drug addiction and yet still disagree on
the relevance of these "facts" in the present case.

We can see from the example how background theories bear
on particular judgments about particular cases. First, these larger
theoretical conceptions are *both* normative and factual. Second,
it seems implausible to hold that the background conceptions
deployed in the particular case can be used to "deduce" or somehow entail particular judgments about what to do. The virtue of
using Toulmin's model is that we can properly view disputes such
as the one presented in the example as disputes at the level of
attempts to establish different warrants. Moreover, the "backings"
used to "establish" these warrants are complex conceptions that
do not deductively "entail" a certain warrant but rather makes
plausible differing sorts of warrants. We might trace out a whole

family of interconnected warrants that could be classified in terms of the larger background ideals, conceptions, and theories that serve as their "backing."

But what, it might be asked, is the lesson of this example with respect to the possibility of rationally defending views in moral argument? First, it is unclear on the basis of this one example to what extent we would be pressed to formulate some new norm or warrant that could accommodate and resolve these sorts of conflicts. We might for example find it plausible to "officially" employ a norm that says "in cases such as these, we ought to provide the patient with the best available information reflecting the pros and cons of either treatment policy, leaving the final decision to him or her." Of course, this policy may not always be viable. (What if the patient is too incapacitated to make such a determination? Maybe next of kin should then be notified. But what if they are not available?) It all depends on how deeply and frequently these sorts of interpretive conflicts occur.

Secondly, the example might suggest that in some cases, conflicts over warrants are sometimes *appropriate,* perhaps even desirable. Conflict among practitioners in some enterprise might be a sign of vitality. Nevertheless, we do need some agreement on baselines in order for subsidiary conflicts to be permissible and perhaps—in some instances—even desirable.

Thirdly, explicit recognition of interpretive conflicts about "hard" cases might tend to enhance the quality of debate and deliberation. If people realize that in some instances conflict over norms or warrants is the result of differing "warrant-establishing interpretive standpoints," then they will be more likely to work toward mutual understanding in these areas of dispute. I am, of course, assuming that people experiencing such conflicts are willing to accept the claims that moral norms really can become problematic, and therefore that particular moral judgments are fallible. Inculcating habits of open-mindedness about moral matters is itself a persistent challenge for moral education.

The example shows how what seems to be a very narrowly circumscribed problem—what pain medication to provide this ailing patient in these circumstances—actually involves much larger value considerations. To be sure, these doctors do not have the time or occasion to settle these larger questions about the place of human beings in nature and the appropriate level of technological manipulation of natural processes. But *we* who have this case before us can use the example to promote reflection on these larger questions. In fact we can review a whole range of cases that bear on such questions. This might, if properly conducted, be a very useful exercise, which will inevitably have implications for our concrete practice and policy choices.

In the next chapter, I develop an account of the moral domain. The theory of moral knowledge and moral argument developed in this chapter is a theory about the *structure* of these phenomena. As a pragmatist reconstruction, it is both a description of what we do find in practice and a recommendation for how we can systematically think *better* about moral argument and knowledge. Nevertheless, it would be wrong to judge this account by the standards sometimes applied to traditional moral theories like utilitarianism. Part of the point of pragmatism is that we should not expect success in efforts to formulate a moral geometry consisting of moral principles from which we can deduce particular moral judgments. At best, the idea of "applying principles" captures the routine situation in which moral norms are satisfactory. That said, I acknowledge that pragmatists working in ethics and value theory can refine, extend, and develop the implications of the structural account defended here. This would require taking up specific moral problems, as well as engaging in inquiries in moral psychology and social theory. These topics go beyond the scope of what I can treat in this book.

4 | *The Boundaries and Authority of Morality: A Pragmatist View*

The Moral Domain

MORAL NORMS AS RESPONSIBILITIES FOR RELATIONSHIPS

The claims advanced so far are about the structure of practical reasoning and moral rationality, but I have not addressed the question of what counts as "moral." In this chapter, I advance an account of the moral domain that is divided into two parts. In the first section, I offer some suggestions for how to understand what makes a norm "moral." The second section deals with one particular feature that seems to separate moral from nonmoral norms: the special authority or force of moral considerations.

Pragmatism takes norms or habits to be absolutely central to human life and practical reasoning. Obviously, not all norms are moral. Norms that compose domains like cooking, music, and medicine must in some way be different from moral norms like truth-telling, prohibitions against killing, gratitude, and the like. My view is that one distinctive mark of moral norms is that they involve responsibilities for relationships.[1] Note that moral norms can be expressed in terms of a three-part relation: the agent who is responsible, the recipient (that to whom the responsibility is due), and a value or good (that which the agent is responsible for with regard to the recipient). Consider the following types of responsibilities:

(1)   We (agents) have a collective responsibility for providing clean air (value) to future generations (recipient). We (agents) have a collective responsibility to distribute healthcare on the basis of need alone (value); (recipient implied: the needy).

(2)   Law enforcement officials (agents) have a responsibility not to obtain information by torturing (value) their prisoners (recipients).

(3)   A parent (agent) has a responsibility for leaving work early in order to care for (value) a sick child (recipient).

(4)   Any person (agent) has a responsibility not to cause unnecessary suffering (value) to any being (recipient) that can feel pain.

(5)   Any person (agent) has a responsibility not to kill (value) innocent people (recipient).[2]

Responsibilities can range from the formal, like those of a circuit court judge, to the informal, like those of a friend.[3] Each relationship harbors specific values. An understanding of what the relationship is—what values and interests it serves—is necessary to understand the responsibilities, including how they ought to be discharged. What it means to be a good parent depends heavily on particular circumstances: the character, financial situation, work life, and so on of the family members. These circumstances can change, so we need to be responsive to these changes. Thus, we can see that the notion of responsibilities for social relationships accommodate both particularism and change of norms—features of norm use identified earlier in the book. Not all responsibilities are "moral" (a person might have legal responsibilities distinct from the moral). In what follows I will try to fill out the pragmatist understanding of what makes responsibilities moral.

THE DEFINITION OF MORALITY: SOME DISTINCTIONS

The question of what defines "morality" is multiply ambiguous because there are several questions we might raise about the moral domain, each of which assumes a different sense of "moral definition." First, there is the question of the *formal definition* of morality. What defines whether a principle, judgment, norm, or ideal counts as moral? Note that answers to the formal question do not judge which moral values are superior.

The formal question can have two further senses. We might be asking about which *philosophical* proposal regarding the definition of morality is best. This kind of question involves inquiry that is in some respects "normative," though not in the sense of "morally good." We might be seeking a definition of morality that is good insofar as it fits in with other established theories such as psychology, sociology, biology, and anthropology. The second sense of the formal question is, "What do people in a society claim defines whether a norm or principle counts as moral?" Answers to this question require sociological or anthropological inquiry.

Consider now a different kind of question about the moral domain: "What should the content of morality be?" Or, put slightly differently: "What obligations are included in the system of morality that we ought to adopt?" Typically, philosophers answer this question by proposing normative ethical theories. Utilitarians claim that the content of morality reduces to one supreme principle: maximize overall good. Kantians claim that the content of morality ought to be derived from one supreme moral law: the categorical imperative.

Notice that philosophers may disagree sharply about what the content of morality ought to be and yet agree on answers to the formal question of what features a norm must possess if it is to count as moral. For example, utilitarians and Kantians might agree that the formal definition of morality includes the following: (1) Moral judgments must be universalizable. (2) Moral principles and judgments reflect an "impartial point of view" in which people no longer give special weight to their own interests. They treat every interest "equally."

There is a second kind of substantive question one might ask regarding the definition of morality: What do people in a society accept as the content of morality? What principles, norms, or values do they profess to believe in? After this question is answered, one might inquire about the extent to which the society actually conforms to its professed morality. In any case, it should be clear that this kind of question is, like the second sense of the formal question, answered through social inquiry. This sense of the "moral domain" is what philosophers commonly refer to as "positive morality."

Finally, we have an important question about moral domain that asks, Who ought to be given moral consideration? Or, put slightly differently, Who should be considered a "moral subject"— an entity to whom moral agents directly owe moral regard? This question too has its sociological counterpart: Who is given moral consideration in a particular society? This kind of question is important for moral debates regarding topics such as the environment, nonhuman animals, and abortion. These areas of ethics deal with questions about "moral status"—questions about who is the proper target of moral obligations. Obviously, the answer to this question does not exhaust the substantive question about which obligations should be fulfilled. Even if we can identify the subjects of obligations, we would still need an account of the content and nature of the obligations owed to these subjects.

To sum up, we have the following categories of moral domain:

(1) Formal definition of morality:
   (a) Philosophical: What definition of what makes a norm "moral," should we adopt?
   (b) Sociological: What definition of what makes a norm "moral" do people in a given society in fact adopt?
(2) Substantive definition of morality:
   (a) Philosophical: What should the content of morality be? What obligations are included in the best moral system?
   (b) Sociological: What is the content of morality in a given society? What obligations do people in a society profess to accept? To what extent does their behavior conform to their stated beliefs?
(3) Substantive definition of moral subjects:
   (a) Philosophical: Who should be given moral direct moral consideration?
   (b) Sociological: Who is given direct moral consideration in a given society?

Pragmatism is skeptical that the substantive questions can be answered definitively or completely, given the contingent nature of our world. Pragmatism denies that any single-principle moral theory can do justice to the pluralism of values, the susceptibility of our practices to change, and the fact that our judgments must be sensitive to the particulars of the situation. We ought to be mindful of the ever-present possibility of problematic situations that require that we regard moral reasoning as an educational process.

The open-ended nature of our substantive moral obligations supports a pragmatist interpretation of "moral obligation" claims that parallels claims about "good" in Chapter 2. Recall that in addition to its warranting use as a predicate of action plans that figure in conclusions of deliberations, "good" is also a shorthand term for heterogeneous internal goods that are fully appreciated and understood by perspicuous inspection of norm-governed activities. The same duality seems to characterize "ought." The warranting use of "ought" functions as a predicate of an action plan. The summary use of "ought" functions to indicate heterogeneous responsibilities whose meaning and import can only be fully understood by careful inspection of the specific relationships in which they function. As a predicate of an action plan, "ought" may be used either in determination or decision problems. In determination problems, we are tentative about the obligation claim attached to the action plan. In decision problems, action plans are settled, and the troubles that may occur are with plan implementation, not plan formulation.

When I defend a claim about a particular obligation such as "I have an obligation to tell my friend my honest opinion about her decision to quit college," this particular obligation is akin to the warranting use of "good." The "ought" in this statement functions in the conclusion of a piece of reasoning. On the other hand, we may use obligation claims in a different way, such as in the judgment: "In general, friends have obligations to give honest opinions to each other." Our understanding of friendship, and its internal goods, involves understanding the kinds of obligations that come attached to the relationship. Pragmatism does not deny that we can offer meaningful, reasonable answers to the substantive moral questions. It is skeptical of attempts to reduce all obligations to a single kind. Given that we live in a changing world with conflicting practices and activities, we need to take an open-minded attitude toward our substantive obligations.

Pragmatists can agree to basic universalization constraints on moral judgments (a point that we made in Chapter 3 in connection to Jonsen and Toulmin's casuistry). Moreover, pragmatists can offer an ideal of impartiality in moral judgment that enjoins us to be continually open to the changing plurality of concrete goods at stake in any deliberative event. These two formal features, universalizability and impartiality, apply to explicit moral reasoning. Since pragmatism holds that norms or habits are concrete ways of thinking, feeling, and doing, a moral norm must be more than its formulation in reasoning about action plans. Moral norms are embedded in practices and activities, and they are in continuous relation with other nonmoral norms. In what follows, I will offer suggestions about characteristics that distinctively apply to moral norms understood in the widest pragmatist sense as habits of thinking, feeling, and doing. I have already suggested one salient feature of moral norms: the fact that they involve responsibilities for relationships. The hypothesis that follows is a first effort to offer an answer to the formal question of the definition of morality. The hypothesis, if good, ought to make sense of our ordinary moral views, and it should help our moral thinking.

One more preliminary point. Much philosophical debate about the formal definition of morality centers on the question of whether the correct account builds some social element into its definition of morality.[4] To the extent that pragmatism begins with the assumption that moral theorizing arises from reflection on conflicts and problems in social practices, it agrees with those who affirm that the formal definition of morality involves a social element. Philosophers who oppose this view argue for a broader conception of the moral that would include norms or ideals that have some kind of priority even though they may not involve a person's relationships to others. In this broader account, the norms that express my devotion to a deity would count as moral insofar as they involve what I take to be supreme commitment. This supreme commitment is expressed by the fact that it will override and prioritize other norms in the person's life.[5] I do not deny that people sometimes accept important life-projects that do not directly impact or involve the interests of others.[6] I believe, however, that the broader approach is too open ended. Many philosophers who think something is radically amiss with morality assume a social definition of morality. When it comes to debates with such "immoralists," the broader account does not seem to do justice to what it is that they object to in the system of "morality."

SOME GENERIC PROPERTIES OF MORAL NORMS

Moral norms comprise what Hegel calls an "ethical substance" in the sense that they exist *in* practices and activities as ways of thinking, feeling, and doing. We can identify them by observing the practices of a community, in much the same way as we can identify religious, aesthetic, and political norms. The responsibilities for social relationships that count as moral tend to be *important*. Without them a community could not function as a unit, nor could it function in relation to other communities. Because moral norms are so important for social living, communities find ways of intentionally inculcating their members to take morality seriously. Nevertheless, an entire community may have responsibilities that it ignores or simply fails to notice. This is no more mysterious than the straightforward idea that a community at some time in its history may ignore the plight and suffering of its elderly, only to later come to see that it has responsibilities to provide for this group of citizens. What follows are characteristics that seem to characterize moral norms:

(1)   Adherence to the norm involves the regulation of social conduct or social interactions.

(2)   The norm tends to function in a variety of practical activities but is itself unstructured in relation to other moral norms.[7]

(3)   The norm tends to be important for the sustained functioning

of an activity or practice, and it is important for regulating the simultaneous pursuit of many activities and practices, especially the possible conflicts between these activities.

(4)   Those who comply with the norm have dispositions to praise compliance and blame violations. These dispositions tend to be based on psychological states such as sympathetic feelings for others—dispositions that are important components of the moral norm itself.

(5)   Sincere adherence to the norm tends to be a basic part of a person's self-identity.

Point 1 is simply a statement that moral norms apply to the regulation of some kind of social conduct or interaction. This is also true of language, political, etiquette, and game norms. What makes moral norms different than others is that moral norms tend to be much broader in scope. They regulate or govern interactions between disparate communities, social practices, and groups. Even more importantly, they typically function to regulate conflicts between various social practices and activities. Second, the violation of moral norms tends to be a more serious matter than the violation of the others. To be sure, violations of language norms can be quite disastrous. But more often than not, the disaster consists in the violation of other basic moral norms required for the use of language norms. If I use words in a different sense than you do and fail to alert you to that fact, I violate a language norm and the moral norm of honesty.

Point 2 is that moral norms are unstructured in relation to each other and have no "home" in a particular practice in the way that most practical norms do. The norms that comprise music-playing have a kind of structure in relation to each other. They are "bound" together in their role of realizing the characteristic purposes of an activity. As Wallace puts it, "The norms that comprise morality . . . because they do not together govern a particular practice, are not so adjusted to one another. Their adjustment comes when they are observed in the pursuit of a particular activity, when they are adjusted to all of the other norms that pertain to the pursuit of that particular activity. It is the particular activity that structures the norms; the norms on the list that

comprise morality are in that respect unstructured in their relation to one another."[8]

Like other norms or habits, moral norms display the three
traits: transmission, interpenetration, and transaction. Given the
claim that moral norms are unstructured in relation to each other,
their fundamental character as norms with these three dimensions is likely to be misunderstood. We are more likely, for example,
to think of cooking norms as historically evolving entities, impacted
by other practical considerations and circumstances, precisely because cooking is a relatively well-defined practice. We are less likely
to think the same about morality because moral norms are unstructured. Thus it is understandable that people have thought
of morality as a list of timeless, practice-independent principles.
It is easier to abstract moral norms from particular practices and
activities because they do in fact range wide across many domains of human life. When we consider the fact that morality
plays such a fundamental role in both self-identity and the regulation of human conduct, it is even more understandable that
people think of morality in abstraction from evolving practices and activities. First, those who wield social power have a
vested interest in preserving the idea that moral considerations
are beyond time, change, and chance. Second, given the painful
reality of moral conflict and tragedy, it is consoling to think
that behind the face of tragedy some kind of fixed moral reality
exists.

Point 3 seems uncontroversial. If moral norms are anything,
they are important for the vital functioning of the variety of practices and activities that humans pursue. Moral norms perform
this service in a variety of ways. They may set up "boundaries"
between two practices in order to prevent unacceptable conflict.
Or they may carve out procedures for adjudicating conflicts between practices. They may set out regulative strategies for han-
dling determination problems. To be sure, a great diversity of
moral values are compatible with the "survival" of a society. One
can imagine a society that makes life miserable for most of its
members and yet still survives with some minimal moral code
intact. This fact does not defeat my purpose here because I am

not evaluating the content of particular moralities but attempting to flesh out features that characterize moral norms generally.

Point 4 is the claim that people who acquire moral norms acquire dispositions to praise and blame themselves and each other. Given that adherence to moral norms is an important matter for the range of human activities, it is no surprise that societies imbue their members with a "moral conscience"—with a tendency to blame and praise. Consider the differences between craft and moral consciences. A "craft conscience" does typically accompany the pursuit of an activity like art. The artist may scold herself and others for poor work and praise herself and others for good work. The aesthetic conscience is composed of judgments of praise and blame that are directly tied to the norms that comprise good performance in the field. Of course, aesthetic norms are continually being contested and rarely command a stable consensus for long periods of time. Nevertheless, aesthetic judgments of praise and blame are based on some sense of good performance, where good performance can only be fleshed out by goods internal to an activity. Moral praise and blame, on the other hand, are based in norms that are not tied to one particular activity. Moral norms show up in a variety of activities and practices. Thus any activity or practice may become the object of moral judgment. Usually, career choices are not directly or overtly "moral." However, in Jane Addams' case, the decision to found Hull House instead of pursuing a career as a doctor is a deeply moral decision, based on sensitivity to complex social problems. For the pragmatist, any activity may potentially be included in the moral domain.

I am not assuming that moral praise and blame must be accompanied by careful reasoning or deliberation (frequently they are not). Nor am I claiming that the practice of praise and blame is always productive. Dewey argues that the tendency to praise and blame frequently inhibits good moral reasoning. The emotional heat generated by praise and blame gets in the way of careful and critical thinking. It also leads to a kind of defensiveness that saps energy better spent examining the conditions and consequences of the moral problem.[9] My distinction between determination and decision problems helps here. Oftentimes we rush to frame a problem as a decision problem and thus engage in heated praise and blame. If the problem is really a determination problem, then Dewey is right to remind us that we waste time in hurdling blames.

Hume's moral philosophy locates moral praise and blame in deep-seated psychological capacities, especially the capacity for what he calls "sympathy."[10] "Sympathy" is not a criterion for moral judgment, nor does it, in this context, refer to a particular moral norm. Rather, sympathy is a fundamental psychological capacity that makes morality possible. It is beyond the scope of this book to pursue the nature and character of these capacities. However, inquiry into their nature is an important task because one enduring challenge any community faces is the question of how best to foster psychological capacities like sympathy.

Finally, consider point five. Moral norms are responsibilities for relationships that play an important role in a person's *identity*. This does not mean that the person who tells the truth views truth-telling *per se* as the most important part of her life but that moral norms like truth-telling, gratitude, and charity are vital components of her activities and practices. My identity as a father is intimately bound up with my identification with my family. My understanding of family life and its internal goods is inseparable from an understanding of moral norms like truth-telling, gratitude, and patience.

The pragmatist formal account of the moral domain is set out as a hypothesis that not only aids our understanding of morality but also helps us to think *better* about moral matters. Obviously, it does not fully accord with the understanding of "common sense" morality insofar as common sense sometimes harbors the belief that moral authority resides in some transhuman realm. Nor does this view accord with that part of commonsense morality that is radically subjectivist about ethics. Pragmatism thinks that morality is "objective" not just in the sense that we can locate patterns of behavior and belief that people call "moral" but also in the sense that moral norms, like other practical norms, reside in norm-governed practices that transcend the lives of particular people.

Authority of Moral Norms

Many philosophers maintain that moral considerations have a special authority that other practical considerations lack. Morality is a domain of important values that trump other kinds of values. Moral considerations have an authority that should weigh heavily in our practical deliberations. Pragmatism views the norms of morality as interpenetrating with other nonmoral norms. Thus, although moral norms do have a special importance, they do not comprise a domain of activity separate from the nonmoral activities and practices of communities. The pragmatist answer that I defend is that the authority of moral norms is grounded in the fact that they express responsibilities for important social ties and relationships. We find ourselves born into ties and relationships—morality is "built into" these. Grounding the authority of moral norms in contingent facts about the social nature of human life might appear inadequate. After all, if moral claims express "contingent truths" that might be otherwise, how can we maintain that they have a special "necessity" or "force"? Dewey has a neat reply to those who would complain that the mere fact that morality is a contingent part of human life does not answer the question of *why* we ought to take it seriously. Dewey argues that the same question could be asked with the same force for theories that view morality as transcendent of human practices. Dewey writes:

> What claim have they [moral standards] upon us? In one sense, the question is unanswerable. In the same sense, however, the question is unanswerable whatever origin and sanction is ascribed to moral obligations and loyalties. Why attend to metaphysical and transcendental ideal realities even if we concede they are the authors of moral standards? Why do this act if I feel like doing something else? Any moral question may reduce itself to this question if we so choose.

But in an empirical sense the answer is simple. The authority is that of life. Why employ language, cultivate literature, acquire and develop science, sustain industry, and submit to the refinements of art? To ask these questions is equivalent to asking: Why live? And the only answer is that if one is going to live one must live a life of which these things form the substance. The only question having sense which can be asked is *how* we are going to use and be used by these things, not whether we are going to use them. Reason, moral principles cannot in any case be shoved behind these affairs, for reason and morality grow out of them. But they have grown into them as well. . . . In short, the choice is not between a moral authority outside of custom and one within it. It is between adopting more or less intelligent and significant customs.[11]

Now, the worry about "force" or "authority" of moral norms may not be so much about its metaphysical status as it is about human failure to comply with, or respect, moral rules. A basic goal of moral education is to instill habits that insulate its students from decision problems. The pragmatist need not deny that failure to follow moral rules is a reality with which any human community must deal.

DEWEY'S THEORY OF DUTY

The reply just given to the skeptic's "why" question is negative, challenging the questioner to admit that pragmatism is not especially prone to its bite. However, pragmatism can offer positive suggestions about "authority." The trick is to find an account of moral authority that does some justice to the supposed "force" behind moral rules yet also accommodates the pragmatist claim that in principle no moral rule should be immune to possible criticism. We can find much insight by taking a close look at Dewey's theory of "right" in his 1932 *Ethics*. Dewey's account of right is meant to capture what he regards as partially correct insights of deontological theories of obligation. Dewey thinks that deontology, consequentialism, and virtue ethics are all partial truths about ethics that need to be combined into one theory that includes "three independent factors of morals." Although I agree with this value pluralism, I am not following Dewey's own intent in focusing on the connection between obligation and social relationships. Dewey seems to consign the connection to relatively well-developed relationships between individuals. My aim is to capture the authority of *all* moral requirements in terms of different kinds of relationships. With that caveat in mind, I turn more closely to his text.

Dewey holds that the "right" as a moral category should not be reduced away to arbitrary commands or desires. Nor should the "right" be thought of in reductively instrumental terms, as when we view all obligation claims as mere means to satisfy narrow egoist desires. Rather, obligation claims arise out of, and reinforce, relationships that contribute to basic interests. Dewey puts it this way: "Right, law, duty, arise from the relations which human beings intimately sustain to one another, and their authoritative force springs from the very nature of the relation that binds people together."[12]

Obligations in general are built into norm-governed activities that make possible various internal values and goods.[13] People can use obligation claims to express judgments about the proper pursuit of a practice or activity. These obligation claims are tied to the very nature of the relationship at issue, so they do not need to be justified by reference to some property of obligation outside all relationships. Nor are these obligation claims the arbitrary expressions of will. Dewey writes, "A child may be subject to demands from a parent which express nothing but the arbitrary wish of the latter, plus a power to make the child suffer if he does not conform. But the claims and demands to which a child is subject need not proceed from arbitrary will; they may issue from the very nature of family life in the relation which exists between parent and offspring."[14] He goes on to say later, "The duties which express these relations are intrinsic to the situation, not enforced from without. The one who becomes a parent assumes by that very fact certain responsibilities. Even if he feels these to be a burden and seeks to escape from them, he flees something which is part of himself and not from something imposed by external force."[15]

The same could be said for other social relationships such as friendship, political office, religious institutions, and so on. Such relationships involve "claims" or "demands" that are intrinsic to the relationship. At least one party in the relationship must be able to conceive of herself as a responsible moral agent who makes and receives demands. However, cases regarding the claims of children and other sentient nonrational beings demonstrate that it is not always true that concerned parties are able to articulate these demands or to have conceptions of their role in the relationship.

Dewey claims that although the existence of right *in general* is plausibly connected to the fact that right claims support and make possible social relations, it does not follow that particular right claims are correct:

> "While particular rights and duties may, then, be arbitrary there is nothing arbitrary or forced in the existence of right and obligation. The Romans spoke of duties as *offices*. An office is a function which has a representative value; that is, it stands for something beyond itself. It is as a parent, not just an isolated individual, that a man or woman imposes obligations on children; these grow out of the office or function the parent sustains, not out of mere personal will. When they express merely one will in opposition to another . . . they violate their own basis."[16]

We can better interpret Dewey's idea in the light of our theory of the duality of "ought" claims. The summary use of "ought" claims derives from normative conceptions of the social ties in which such obligations are based (e.g., a *good* family). These general conceptions may change over time in response to deliberate problem solving or simply through other causal factors. At any given time, general "ought" claims may be dubious (for example, the claim that women should not be politically enfranchised). On the other hand, an "ought" claim may be arbitrary *relative to some particular action plan,* although the general obligation upon which it is founded may be quite sound. For example, a person may be correct that, in general, doctors have an obligation to save lives, but a particular patient may be in such great pain, with no chance to live longer, that it is better not to save his life. In such a case, many believe that the appropriate action plan would be to painlessly kill the patient. The obligation to preserve life would not be the appropriate "ought" claim in the action plan for treating this particular case.

GENERALIZED NORMS

I have sketched an account that locates the authority of moral norms in the intrinsic connection between such norms and the social roles and relationships. This does not mean that any norm that happens to be linked to any social role is justified. It does mean that when we criticize "ought" claims in general or in particular action plans, we should do so by appeal to an *interpretation* of what a role or relationship *ought to be*. Moral interpretation need not make reference to some role-independent notion of "right in general," but rather it may refer to some specific understanding of what a concrete social relation ought to be in light of an understanding of the goods that the social relation makes possible.[17] (In the next chapter, I will try to show how such interpretation plays out in the communication communities that practice social criticism.)

We may grant that moral norms are internally connected to concrete social relations but still wonder whether increasingly abstract perspectives might be adopted—perspectives independent of concrete social relations. In short, isn't it possible to abstract from the concrete function that a moral norm plays in some specific social relation and view it as governing a whole range of social relations? True, a norm such as "be faithful to those that you represent" might apply in the context of the social relations between a union and its representatives. However, it seems obvious that this norm applies to "all unions and their representatives" and can be further generalized to all organizations who elect or appoint representatives. Paralleling the increasing abstractness of moral norms might be increasingly abstract "self-descriptions." To take a "developmental" example, it might be that a child learns to tell the truth in the context of the family life, with its particular internal goods. But over time she learns how to follow the truth-telling norm in an array of contexts outside of her family life.

This point about the capacity to generalize moral norms and moral self-descriptions may be granted, but with some important qualifications. First, it is true that by formulating moral norms in general terms we are capable of formulating principles of judgment that are serviceable in a variety of contexts. The pragmatist may grant that in their use as regulative principles, it is often very useful to formulate moral norms in very general terms that can be applied in a variety of situations. Dewey makes this point in the following:

> At first, duties are connected with specific relations, like those of a child to his parents, to his brothers and sisters. But with increased moral maturity, there develops a sense of obligation in distinction from any particular situation. While a general idea arises of recurrence of special situations, it is more than a mere extract from them. It constitutes a new attitude toward further special situations. A person may use a variety of things in succession as if they were tables. When he has the general idea of a table, he is in possession of a *principle* of action. He can use this idea as an ideal, as something by which to criticize existing tables, and by which, under changed conditions, to invent a new table. . . . So a person with a general conception of duty will have a new attitude; he will be on the lookout for situations in which the idea applies. He will have an ideal or standard to which he must bring up particular cases.[18]

Dewey makes the important point that the formulation of general principles of action provide us with critical ideals that can be used to judge new cases. A generalized principle is a regulative ideal. Thus, generalizing moral norms into regulative principles can be of important use in determination problems. The attitude change that agents experience when they use moral norms as regulative principles involves a willingness to reflectively revise norms in light of new circumstances and unforeseen conflicts.[19]

Dewey goes on to mention *another* distinct use of the generalized sense of right, namely, that it helps to prevent moral agents from temptations to dodge obligations. It seems fairly clear that Dewey is talking about the way general moral norms assist in overcoming or avoiding decision problems. Dewey writes:

> The proper function of a general sense of duty is to make us sensitive to the relations and claims involved in particular situations, and this sensitiveness is especially needed whenever some immediate solicitation of desire tends to blind us to everything but itself. A generalized sense of right is a support in times of temptation; it gives a reinforcing impetus in carrying us over a hard place in conduct. A mother is habitually attentive to the claims of her offspring. Nevertheless, cases arise when it is much easier to put her own comfort first. A generalized sense of right and obligation is a great protection; it makes the general habit consciously available. But such a general sense as this grows out of occasions when the mother was faithful because she was actuated by a direct affection for the child and direct interest in his welfare. A sense of duty is a weak staff when it is not the outcome of a habit formed in whole-hearted recognition of the value of the ties involved in the concrete case.[20]

Dewey rejects the notion that the generalized sense of duty is somehow independent of human desires, good, and welfare. The sense of duty is animated by habits that are informed by a care for certain interests (such as the parent's concern for the welfare of a child). Another way of putting the point is that the general sense of duty helps to situate particular desires in a wider context of conduct, thereby educating us about the meaning of our desires so that we can better deal with decision problems.[21]

MORAL NONCONFORMITY

One objection to my account is that it seems to reduce the "individual" into the roles or functions that she plays in some social context. Is there no room for autonomy, for an individual to change or evacuate her social roles? In reply, we should first grant that an individual can evacuate a particular social role, but we deny that she can escape all social roles and relationships. Genuine individuality arises out of social relations.[22] Moreover, moral nonconformity can be an important value once we grant the pragmatist hypothesis that moral norms are contingent habits. Moral nonconformists sometimes turn out to be those who have changed some practice, institution, or social relation for the better. But these nonconformists are justified insofar as their violation of extant norms turns out to benefit the community life. Thus their attempts to violate some social role or put it to new uses are clearly distinguished from the use of a social role for private egoist gain. The moral nonconformist, Dewey writes, "is implicitly putting forth a social claim, something therefore to be tested and confirmed by further trial by others. He therefore recognizes that when he protests he is liable to suffer the consequences that result from his protestings; he will strive with patience and cheerfulness to convince others."[23] Immediately following this passage, Dewey argues that if the moral nonconformist must be willing to accept the negative consequences of his activity, moral conformists must strive to cultivate toleration of such nonconformity:

> History shows how much of moral progress has been due to those who in their own time were regarded as rebels and treated as criminals. . . . Toleration is thus not just an attitude of good humored indifference. It is the positive willingness to permit reflection and inquiry to go on in the faith that the truly right will be rendered more secure through questioning and discussion, while things which have endured merely from custom will be amended or done away with. Toleration of difference in moral judgment is a duty which those most insistent upon duty find it hardest to learn. . . . [W]ithout freedom of thought and expression of ideas, moral progress can occur only accidentally and by stealth. Mankind still prefers upon the whole to rely on force, not now exercised directly and physically like it was once, but upon covert and indirect force, rather than upon intelligence to discover and cling to what is right.

One higher-order responsibility that communities have is to support, or at least tolerate, the activities of social critics—especially those nonconformists who challenge our current conceptions and practices. Dewey almost suggests that moral criticism is inevitable and that even if a society attempts to suppress it by force, it will happen covertly. Even if Dewey's observation is overly optimistic, written as it was in 1932 before full experience of totalitarian regimes that followed just a few years later, it nonetheless expresses a sound pragmatist ideal: good communities ought to create an environment in which open discussion and debate help us to learn about determination problems. Good social critics should accept that their responsibility is primarily to the communities to whom they belong. This means that they be willing to express their criticisms in ways that draw on common, shared moral understandings. It also means that they adopt a certain humility toward their vocation—that they be willing to accept rejection.

The next chapter works out an account of social criticism as undertaken by the local critic who communicates to democratically organized publics. Notice that we have come full circle to the point made in the introduction: pragmatist moral theory arises out of the need to reconstruct of cultural practices. The moral theorist and social critic ought to be engaged in the common enterprise of helping a community better understand its responsibilities and thereby improve its practices.

Given that determination problems are genuine features of moral life, then the best way to deal with them is in open, free discussion and debate. Moral theory and social criticism are activities that, in their own unique ways, exist because there are such determination problems. Pragmatism emphasizes that a large part of moral life is an education process. This process, the pragmatist claims, is accomplished more effectively when it is carried out with an honest understanding that morality is an evolving, shared enterprise.

Finally, to say that morality is "evolving" is not to say that it is a process working toward a fixed and finished goal. Morality "evolves" in ways more like Darwin's notion of evolution as "descent with modification." Moral habits are continually modified to cope with changing "niches."[24] This modification is sometimes intelligent, sometimes unreflective. Pragmatists work to make criticism of moral norms more intelligent so that they may be modified to better practices in the here and now. Such a view of moral improvement can only be called "meliorism."

5 | *Pragmatist Social Criticism*

The final chapter is devoted to demonstrating that the pragmatist theory of morality should interface with a robust social criticism. The metaethical job performed in this book is concerned mostly with rather conceptual goals. These involve the negative task of unseating theoretical obstacles that hamper a clear recognition of the importance of habits for understanding the nature of morality. On the positive side, we have shown the ways in which our theory of habits helps us better understand moral knowledge and reasoning. As "conceptual" as these issues may be, for pragmatists critical reconstruction of concepts is itself an exercise in habits of thinking that have become reflective about themselves and that are indirectly linked to practices and activities. This claim should not be underestimated. If the pragmatist account of practical reason, moral knowledge, and moral domain is correct, then we have vindicated the Dewey claim made in the introduction that moral theory is simply an extension of what we are already doing in our everyday lives when practices and activities conflict or become problematic. For the pragmatist, morality does not reside in some mysterious transcendent realm independent of our created contingent practices, nor is it an expression of merely personal sentiment. Moral considerations are responsibilities developed in community.

To be sure, metaethics is not likely to play a major role in changing the attitudes of the larger culture. Few would regard moral theorizing to be much more than a necessary, and far from a sufficient, condition for reconstruction of moral beliefs and practices. Nevertheless, pragmatist moral theory can play a distinctive role in helping philosophers reconstruct their own self-image and thereby at least indirectly help the philosophical community bring its special skills and talents to bear on social criticism. This should be clear when we keep in mind that the pragmatist view defended in this book is as much a metaphilosophical account of the *nature of moral theory* as it is an account of the status and authority of morality as it exists in social practices. If the pragmatist view is correct, then what all moral theorists are "really" doing, in even the most metaethical inquiries, is treating the intellectual tools generated by moral problem solving in practices and activities. Obviously, moral philosophers do not frequently think of their theoretical activities in this way. So this claim is controversial because it violates their self-understanding. The implications of this pragmatist view are more profound than raising ire in nonpragmatist philosophers who may (with some justice) be offended at being told what they are really up to when they think about morality. The pragmatist metatheory of moral theory would make it hard to resist the view that the tools of moral philosophy ought to be used to help in the process of social reconstruction. In some sense, that is what these "tools" are for. Therefore, the moral philosopher ought to forge conceptual tools more deliberately with the aim of assisting the social critic.[1] The tools forged in this book have mainly concerned the formal properties of moral norms and moral reasoning. They are meant to be relatively "all-purpose" in the sense that they help organize our thinking about the range of issues in moral life. In this respect, my pragmatist theory is not offered for the sole purpose of treating difficult problems in social ethics such as abortion, the environment, and issues of death and dying. Nevertheless, pragmatists like Dewey take seriously the philosopher's responsibility for evaluating current social problems. It is important that we at least sketch the connection between the formal account and the process of social criticism. This chapter will offer that sketch. The point, therefore, of developing the connection between pragmatist moral theory and social criticism is two-fold. First, it illustrates that pragmatist moral philosophy entails a social responsibility for philosophers that is not frequently acknowledged by nonpragmatists. The very antipragmatist conception of moral theorizing as a self-contained professional activity is, no doubt, a large part of why philosophers do not typically acknowledge broader social responsibilities tied to their theorizing. Second, the pragmatist account of social criticism provides further evidence for the value of its approach to moral theory by demonstrating how its theoretical constructs can improve our understanding of moral debate about vexing social problems.

The first part of the chapter will offer a brief defense of an ideal of social criticism as a communication between the local critic (one of us) and democratically organized communities.[2] The best social criticism is criticism in which members of communities work together to produce deliberative events that resolve common problems in light of free social inquiry involving all of the relevant publics. I will offer both moral and epistemological arguments for this ideal, drawing on some ideas of Dewey and Walzer. I conclude the chapter by looking at two examples of social criticism that will help us flesh out some of the implications of the ideal. The examples are Jane Addams' analysis of charity, and the extension of moral concern to nonhuman animals. In both cases, we will be examining how, in many cases, good social criticism involves problematizing taken-for-granted widely shared assumptions rather than offering a simple definitive resolution of every dimension of complex moral problems. The examples will show how social critics can provide useful help in the preliminary interpretation of the problem—the second step in the deliberative event. Obviously, the ethics of social work and the moral status of animals involve arguments about substantive moral obligations that fill books. My purpose in looking at these cases is not to resolve debates about our substantive moral obligations but to demonstrate the ways in which a pragmatist account of social criticism sheds quite a bit of light on the nature of these debates.

Social Criticism as Immanent Critique

THE CRITICS

Deliberative events mediate habits. Some ethical deliberative events may be confined to a relatively short time span and may affect relatively few individuals (e.g., whether divorce is best for a particular family). Yet other deliberative events may involve questions about widely shared social habits. Sometimes the most valuable activities of social critics involve casting new light on shared social habits by questioning hidden or unacknowledged assumptions embedded in these habits. Critics help us to see some bit of social reality *as* a problem. For example, feminist social critics help us to see "personal values" in family life as political values of gender subordination. Marxists demonstrate the ways in which ideals of equality represented in moral rights to property actually advance the interests of powerful economic elites.

Since social critics frequently unearth deep cultural assumptions, they are engaged in the process of "cultural elaboration and affirmation," as Walzer puts it.[3] Walzer points out that "'social criticism' has a pronominal and reflexive function, like 'self–criticism,' which names the subject and object at the same time."[4] This need not imply that *societies* at large criticize themselves (as some sort of "superindividuals"). What this claim means is that individual members of a society, insofar as they practice social criticism, are engaged in reflectively accounting for the practices of a community to a public whose common life, interests, and concerns the critic shares.

The idea that social criticism resembles self-criticism reveals the moral basis of the ideal of the local critic. This moral basis is our sense that it is morally praiseworthy to be critical of oneself before one "cast stones" at others. This sense is tied, perhaps, to our belief that being overconcerned with the failures of others tends to belie a hypocritical refusal to consider one's own faults.

If we probe the matter further, we might put the moral argument for the ideal of the local critic in terms of communal rights and the corresponding duties these rights impose on "outsiders." One might argue that communities have the right to self-determination and self-definition. This right is based in our sense of the value of autonomy. The value of autonomy in turn might be based in the claim that autonomy is tied to the capacity to engage in "self-definition." Freedom involves free self-definition, that is, the capacity to form and pursue self-chosen self-descriptions in the context of one's own community.

The correlative duty on outsiders is to refrain from imposing standards external to the self-understandings of the insiders. Not to respect this duty by engaging in what Walzer calls "disconnected criticism" is to risk a kind of coercion. Walzer puts the point this way:

> The problem with disconnected criticism, and thus with criticism that derives from newly discovered or invented moral standards, is that it presses its practitioners toward manipulation and compulsion. Many, of course, resist the pressure; detachment and dispassion are built-in defenses against it. But insofar as the critic wants to become effective, wants to drive his criticism home . . . he finds himself driven to one or another version of an unattractive politics. . . . His is a kind of asocial criticism, an external intervention, a coercive act, intellectual in form but pointing toward its physical counterpart.[5]

The point is not that detached criticism *must* take the form of a kind of coercive imposition of external norms on a community, but that this is a real danger. Nonetheless, although communal self-determination might indeed be a value, it doesn't seem to be an overriding consideration in every case. Sometimes, the right of self-determination, and all that comes with that right (self-definition, self-criticism, etc.), should be overridden when, say, a community engages in morally reprehensible activities.

AN OBJECTION: DO WE NEED "EXTERNAL STANDARDS"?

Can we talk about morally reprehensible activities if the community refuses to acknowledge any wrongdoing? It seems that the only way we can criticize the internal understandings of a community is to appeal to "external" critical standards. In reply,

I would say first that we might grant the existence of some broad general moral standards that are applicable across cultures. Such broad norms might be not to cause unnecessary pain, not to kill, not to torture, and so forth. These norms would be connected to our most basic sense of what is required to be a fully functioning human being. These norms would still be tied to our "understandings," only here we would be talking about understandings that are *relatively detached* from thicker self-descriptions of one's particular communal attachments. To the extent that these sorts of norms are violated, we might allow for cross-communal criticism.[6]

Secondly, the moral worry about disconnected criticism suggests a regulative ideal of constraining criticism of alien cultures. We have good reason to want the foreign critic to continually strive to locate his criticisms inside local understandings. And this, we might add, will require that the aspiring critic really get to know the culture—to take the time to make it (at least somewhat like) his home. The moral argument for the ideal of the local critic is not meant to legislate in advance when and what criticism is appropriate. It is rather a cautionary ideal that should be continually kept in view. The caution is grounded in real experience of the negative effects of disconnected criticism. (Think, for example, of the myriad attempts of Europeans who settled the New World to coercively convert the "natives" without regard to the self-understandings of the latter.)

Consider the epistemological arguments for this ideal. Any good social criticism requires intimate knowledge of the practices, customs, and local conditions of a society. Moreover, if we assume that social criticism is a kind of immanent critique of the understandings of a community, then it is reasonable to conclude that the local critic will have intimate knowledge of these normative self-understandings. The argument is that whatever norms and ideals we might cherish, the best kind of critic is the critic who "lives among us" because we can count on such a critic to better understand our situation and thus to do a better job of determining what's wrong with us.

But this idea seems trivially obvious if all that it amounts to is the claim that in order to do her critical work, the social critic had better know the "facts" of the society to be subjected to critical scrutiny. Before I criticize a society's income distribution, I had better learn about exactly what that distribution is (in terms of its current state and any discernable trends). I had also better seek out the best going hypotheses from social theory and economics to explain this income distribution. If *this* is all that is meant vis-à-vis "knowledge," it seems doubtful that the critic need be "one of us." Why couldn't someone alien to the society learn such information? In other words, what would growing up in China have to do with me—a U.S. citizen—being able to learn about Chinese income distribution in such a way so that I have adequate knowledge to offer critical suggestions to the Chinese? I may, as a practical matter, need to observe the Chinese system up close, thus requiring that I live there. But certainly this is not always true.

The problem with this last suggestion is that it downplays what is critically at issue here, namely, that the *kind* of knowledge relevant to good social criticism is not simply knowledge of "social facts" but rather a kind of moral knowledge. Moreover, as I argued in Chapter 3, in moral deliberation the choice of certain facts *as relevant facts of the case* is a choice *already guided by normative commitments*. If we think of social criticism as one kind of moral deliberation, then it seems that social critics need to be guided (at least implicitly) by shared value commitments. They will need the requisite moral knowledge when they make judgments about relevant social facts and problems and the appropriate responses. This point complicates matters insofar as part of the data of the social critic will be the moral norms and ideals of a society. This is not to deny that there may be phases of social inquiry in which people in one phase are engaged predominantly in gathering social facts (the activities of the economists and social theorists), while people in other phases of inquiry may be predominantly engaged in evaluation (the activities of journalists, politicians, and activists). But even if there is such a division of labor, we may reasonably assume that the reflective participants in the process of social criticism would be able to see a symbiotic relation between these phases.

Should the social critic share (at least some of) the moral beliefs held by the community criticized? To put the question another way, is it epistemically advantageous for the social critic to share the moral knowledge of those she criticizes? If by "share" we mean "endorse," it seems that the social critic need not share *all* of the moral beliefs of a community. Nevertheless, in order even to engage in a critical discussion with a community, the critic must share some beliefs with her audience. Even though agreement may not be complete, there needs to be enough of it to get discussion off the ground. Now, if such "basal agreement" defines even the rough parameters of a moral community, then we might argue that the social critic must be "one of us" if she is going to engage us in a meaningful discussion.[7]

The Epistemological Case for Democratic Participation

CRITICS VERSUS "EXPERTS"

I turn now to the society that is the target of social criticism. Social meanings are the objects of the critic's efforts, so social criticism is a *communicative endeavor*. Should the communication between critic and society be reciprocal? The picture of "critic as expert" seems to be at odds with the idea that the critic and her society are in reciprocal communication—that they are equal partners in a dialogue. To say that the critic in some way excels in knowledge or insight does not require that we abandon the idea that the proper relation between critic and criticized is communicative and, even more to the point, mutually educative. Consider the analogy of doctor and patient. A good doctor will carefully listen to her patient's descriptions of symptoms. She will, when offering possible diagnoses and regimes of treatment, respect the responses of her patient. She will not "force" treatment on the patient. She will be concerned with the good of the patient and try to do her best to communicate the future consequences of various medical regimes. The good patient, on the other hand, should strive to communicate symptoms clearly, to understand regimes of treatment, and so on. Consider the example of teacher and pupil. The good teacher strives to clearly communicate a body of knowledge or methods for arriving at knowledge. A teacher can register how much is being learned only by listening to the responses of the pupil. A pupil, on the other hand, should continually strive to communicate his or her understanding of the subject matter, to ask questions of the teacher, and so on. Of course these analogies are not complete. For example, the social critic is not concerned with the individual needs of a particular person, but rather with the meanings of values and norms of social groups. But the point is that in some very straightforward sense we can find cases in which "experts" and "clients" are not exactly equal with respect to their insight and knowledge but that they nevertheless engage in mutual communication in order to further ends and values that are of mutual concern.

We must be precise in defining what is meant by "experts" here. The process of social criticism may involve the use of expert knowledge, as when, for example, we call on scientists to determine the likelihood of risk to a certain population of workers requires that certain safety standards be changed. Yet these sorts of experts may not always be the best social critics, although they may sometimes play this role (as when, for example, a scientist becomes involved in questioning the use of the results of her work in chemistry to build weapons). Typically, it is activists, civic leaders, religious figures, journalists, and the like who play the role of social critic by addressing a concerned public with common moral ideas and vividly showing the relevance of those ideas in light of the "facts of the case"—which facts are often based on knowledge gleaned from expert inquirers. In short, even though we may need to draw on various kinds of technical inquiries in order to assess social problems and possible solutions adequately, the social critic and the publics to which this *technical* knowledge may be relevant are usually sufficiently epistemically situated in terms of *moral* knowledge to be able to determine the normative implications of the technical knowledge.

DEWEY'S THEORY OF THE PUBLIC

Following Dewey, I will reconstruct an epistemological argument for democratic participation in the process of social criticism. This democratic participation requires the formation of "publics." Accordingly, I shall first elaborate Dewey's functional account of "publics." For Dewey, a public is not some entity standing above and beyond the various groups that make up a complex society. Rather, publics are groups that have an interest in regulating some sphere of activity whose typical consequences have a wide-ranging and serious impact on society. To begin with, most societies are comprised of a plurality of groups (families, religions, clubs, economic institutions, etc.) that pursue different kinds of goods and values. The activities of these groups involve certain shared interests. Thus, members of these groups typically understand, control, and enjoy the activities and ends characteristic of their group. (The "goods" here should be thought of in terms of the notion of "internal goods" developed in Chapter 2). So, for example, the practices, beliefs, and ways of life of a religious group typically create values that affect only those members immediately involved in the group. However, sometimes the practices and activities of a group involve consequences that indirectly affect other individuals or groups. Consider the example of a small town dominated by a certain Christian sect. Once the activities of this religious group have dire consequences that (systematically) begin to affect others outside the group, a "public" is called into existence. Dewey writes of publics, "The public consists of all those who are affected by the indirect consequences of transactions to such an extent that it is deemed necessary to have those consequences systematically cared for. Officials are those who look out for and take care of the interests thus affected. Since those who are indirectly affected are not direct participants in the transactions in question, it is necessary that certain persons

be set apart to represent them."[8] Dewey thinks that this definition of publics is the best way of accounting for a wide variety of
political activities and practices. The above passage also alludes
to "officials." Dewey's functional definition of publics yields a
functional definition of the state as those publics that are organized by laws, officials, and agencies to care for and regulate activities that have a systematic, indirect impact on a wide variety
of groups.[9]

The notion of a public in its richest sense involves a *communication community,* that is, a group of individuals who mutually
understand certain shared interests and attempt to coordinate
their action to realize these interests.[10] Nonetheless, sometimes
Dewey seems to offer a "passive" conception of publics in the
sense that he seems to claim that publics are simply "brought
about" whenever indirect consequences of some sphere of social
activity affect other individuals or groups. Consider the following passage:

> Indirect, extensive, enduring and serious consequences of conjoint
> and interacting behavior call a public into existence having a com-
> mon interest in controlling these consequences. . . . Such is our the-
> sis regarding the eclipse which the public idea and interest have
> undergone. There are too many publics and too much public con-
> cern for existing resources to cope with. The problem of a demo-
> cratically organized public is primarily an intellectual problem, in a
> degree to which the political affairs of prior ages offer no parallel.[11]

A public may be "called into being" *virtually* in the sense that
some sphere of social activity is not *yet* readily recognized as having dire consequences. The public is "brought into existence" in
the sense that there really is a problem that impinges on basic
interests of people, yet there is little recognition of the scope and
import of the problem. Dewey's claim that there are "too many
publics" seems to mean that there are too many uncoordinated
groups, which get in the way of mutual recognition of common
problems. For example, a group of individuals may be members
of the same economic class, suffering from problems endemic to

that class but failing to see these common problems because of their lack of shared membership in other groups such as religions, race or gender groups, nationalities, and so on. These other group affiliations may obfuscate or confuse what might otherwise be recognized as important shared interests.

Thus, there is no *effectively organized* public until common problems are mutually recognized. Problems may not be fully recognized until various sorts of inquiries are brought to bear on the situation—for example, studies that show the decline of income and the steady erosion of labor rights over a period of time might be used to bring about a self-conscious awareness among the workers. A public that identifies itself is a public that has already been brought to some awareness of an underlying problem. After the problems have been identified, solutions can be offered and tested by such self-conscious publics. Organized publics can help identify further problems.[12] Addams and the settlement house movement illustrate this multi-dimensional role of publics. These houses were a response to widespread urban poverty resulting from industrialization. But they were formed not only to alleviate some of these problems (e.g. providing food, shelter, and other social services) but also to serve as a means of actively inquiring into further problems of urban life in order to formulate more effective responses. The founders of settlement houses explicitly viewed them as "experimental" communities concerned with resolving social problems.

DEWEY'S EPISTEMOLOGICAL ARGUMENT

Dewey claims that we need to take an "experimental" attitude towards the general theories and principles that we bring to bear on social problems. Social inquiry requires that we adopt the fallibilistic attitude appropriate to all inquiry and problem solving. The pragmatist view of moral knowledge that we have defended here follows Dewey in the idea that general principles are useful as tools for resolving determination problems. We can only be confident that we have successfully completed a deliberative event after we implemented some action plan.

But to what extent should the general citizenry participate in experimental inquiry into social problems? It may be that an economist or political scientist would do well to avoid "absolutist" conceptions of social inquiry. But is there any sense to the claim that social inquiry should involve the experimental participation of the *whole* citizenry? What would such experiments look like? Although certain kinds of expert knowledge may not be readily accessible to the citizenry at large, this is not generally true of the kind of moral knowledge required to evaluate social problems and proposed solutions to these problems.[13] Although it may be true that as a practical matter citizens cannot participate in *every* aspect of social inquiry that may bear on their social problems, they nevertheless can and should participate in decisions that bear on their basic interests.

Dewey argues that the masses need to be consulted at the beginning of the process of social inquiry in order to locate and solve social problems effectively. To the extent that the "experts" cut themselves off from the input of the citizenry, they fail to gather knowledge about social problems and ways to respond to them that preserve the common good. Dewey writes, "A class of experts is inevitably so removed from common interests as to become a class with private interests and private knowledge, which in social matters is not knowledge at all."[14] Simply put, to the extent that "experts" claim they are qualified to rule because they better understand social problems and social values, they must consider the input of society at large. To the extent that they do not consider the input of society, any knowledge that they may glean will most likely reflect their own private interests. The proper "object" of social inquiry is *values and norms as they are understood* by a community and the problematic situations that arise in light of these value commitments. That is, it is only by taking account of these understandings that one can determine what values are problematic and what adequate solutions might be. Moreover, open public discussion of social problems will tend to clarify the nature of the problems and facilitate an understanding of which solutions might be adequate. Democratic participation has an epistemic and educative role.[15]

Dewey goes on to offer two further replies to the charge that the masses are too stupid to participate in political decision making. First, he claims that the charge probably exaggerates what is required to make informed political judgments. The lay person may not comprehend all of the engineering facts behind safety features in power plants and the tax scheme that may be required to implement regulation of such industries; however, he does know what it means to be sick from pollution and does have some sense of what would be an acceptable risk of becoming ill. He also has certain basic moral expectations based on the values and norms that he is educated in, which values and norms are the fund of ongoing moral traditions. It is this sort of "value-fact" knowledge that he should be able to express and clarify in the context of democratic publics.

The knowledge relevant to social criticism is fundamentally "moral knowledge." This knowledge is not insulated from the facts of inquiry but is rather in continual symbiotic relation with such inquiry. Our factual inquiries are guided (in part) by our value commitments, and our value commitments may change in light of our factual findings. We may need to find ways to communicate the results of factual inquiry to the citizenry effectively so that they are better able to make informed political and moral judgments.[16] Yet it seems fairly clear that most citizens posses the common moral knowledge that serves as the background for understanding and interpreting the results of factual inquiries. Furthermore, the social critics who draw conclusions on the basis of both moral and factual knowledge will not always be the same people as those experts who conduct factual inquiries (a point I have already made). The social critic will typically be the person skilled at evocative renderings of the meanings of our moral life in light of the best available knowledge about our current circumstances. For that purpose, a good social critic is more like a novelist, poet, or prophet.

Dewey's second point in rebuttal to the charge that citizens are not "smart" enough is that the intelligence is not "fixed" but depends upon social conditions and the level of educational opportunity that such conditions support. The idea, then, would be that until we make better attempts to improve the overall level of education of the general public, we should not draw hasty conclusions about its inability to participate in political decision making.[17]

I have not nearly touched on all of the important areas of democratic theory. My concern is limited to making good the claim that social criticism requires democratic participation. I leave open the possibility of other arguments for democracy, as well as more precise renderings of what sort of democratic arrangements are possible and desirable for our times and circumstances.

In sum, the idea that citizens should be allowed to participate in social inquiry and criticism is not equivalent to the idea that every citizen should participate in every factual inquiry relevant to some social problem. It is rather the idea that citizen input should enter into such inquiries from the beginning (they should be consulted about "where it hurts") and at the end, when the results of such inquiries are communicated and decisions about their relevance and importance need to be made. The view advocated here, however, challenges citizens to take a hypothetical attitude toward moral norms and values. That is, they must be willing to accept that norms need reconstruction in light of new conflicts and changing conflicts. This involves an understanding of moral and political norms as tools that help to reconstruct problematic situations that impinge on shared interests. These same norms, as they are used, will no doubt undergo reconstruction from time to time. Think, for example, of the way that our understanding of the strong right to private property is currently undergoing transformation in response to environmental considerations.

The idea that we should think of political norms as "tools" that grow out of responses to solve social problems and are themselves modifiable during their subsequent use is well expressed in the following passage, in which James Campbell applies this conception to fundamental political conceptions. Campbell writes:

> Rather than seeing these conceptions of political ideas as unchanging verities, it is better to view them as "tools" . . . for refining the material of experience and solving particular problems. Rather than seeing ourselves as attempting to recognize the antecedently "correct" meanings of political terms, we need to see ourselves as attempting to discover what particular terms might best mean within our particular situations. For example, what might a full conception of democracy be in our situation? Here, as elsewhere in existence, there is novelty. New understandings emerge as new experiences are encountered. New situations indicate the weaknesses and inadequacies of our past formulations. . . . The meanings of our key political ideas change, because like other tools, they develop with ongoing use. In the process of problem solution . . . we hammer out a cluster of interdependent conceptions of terms like democracy, liberty, and community with which we can live for the present. Each of these interdependent conceptions is a stage in the evolution of our understandings of these key political ideas, and collectively they form a dialectical and processive whole.[18]

Part of the task of the social critic is to help facilitate the intellectual reconstruction of normative conceptions. Such intellectual reconstruction would involve placing these conceptions in the particular contexts of their use, describing the sorts of problems they might be designed to solve, as well as discussing new problems that require changes in the character of these "tools." We should not be beguiled into an overly rationalistic account of norms such that we view the community of norm users as "designing" solutions to clearly agreed upon problems. Of course, as of now, it is simply not true that this view of norms reflects the "common understanding." By now, it should be obvious that pragmatism is not entirely consistent with the "ordinary understanding" of moral political and values. But one thing is clear, the proposal to think of norms in this pragmatic way does not capture (and is not intended to capture) ordinary understandings. This fact, in itself, is not a flaw of the theory. If the theory completely "violated" ordinary understandings or could never be reflectively endorsed by practitioners, then we would indeed have reason to doubt the theory. But we have no evidence now that this is true.

Second, as has already been mentioned, deliberative events treating complex social problems are frequently so difficult because social critics challenge us to rethink what we take to be problematic. Sometimes this is simply by informing us of factual matters about which we were unaware. For example, documentation of abuse of animals in factory farms may lead many to rethink the morality of eating meat generated through cruel procedures. But sometimes, the more difficult (and more interesting) kinds of distortions involve hidden assumptions that prevent us from seeing a particular activity or practice as problematic.

Genealogy

Given that one important part of social criticism is uncovering distorted moral understandings, it will be useful to conclude the chapter with a brief look at one paradigm of how to achieve critical distance, a "genealogy of morals."[19] I argue that genealogical analysis of moral norms and practices is useful for clarifying such distorted moral self-understandings. By distancing herself from current moral understandings via a critical examination of the historical roots of norm-governed practices, the social critic is frequently able to help clarify distorted current moral understandings. This is often a necessary first step for the more reflexive adjudication of social problems.[20] "Genealogy," as practiced by Foucault and Nietzsche, is often taken to be a skeptical assault on all moral values. I briefly demonstrate why no pernicious skepticism follows from genealogy, once we adopt a pragmatist model of moral reasoning. I conclude by looking at some examples.

As David Couzens-Hoy conceives it,[21] genealogies may be viewed as second-order interpretations of first-order moral interpretations. By tracing out the changes and relations between social practices and the norms that govern these practices, the genealogist seeks to reveal possible misinterpretations involved in our first-order moral interpretations. We begin a genealogical analysis with the acknowledgment that something is awry in our understanding. Putting the point this way makes it seem as if we "recognize" that some moral norm is problematic and only then engage in genealogical inquiry. Yet a genealogy might itself incite us to probe deeper into taken-for-granted moral interpretations. Nietzsche nicely illustrates both points. He talks first about a vaguely felt problem in the first paragraph of *On The Genealogy of Morals* when he speaks of our lack of self-knowledge as not complete ignorance but rather a vague awareness that something has happened to us that we do not yet fully grasp. He compares this vague awareness to hearing a bell that has just struck but that we only notice after the ringing has ceased. Nietzsche writes, "'What really was that which just struck?' so we sometimes rub our ears afterward and ask, utterly surprised and disconcerted, 'what really was that which we have just experienced?' . . . 'who are we really.'"[22] Later it is clear that Nietzsche also believes part of the role of genealogy to be that of *problematizing* taken-for-granted moral interpretations. Nietzsche puts it this way, with regard to the morality of pity: "One has taken the value of these 'values' as given, as factual as beyond all question."[23] Genealogy helps us to see the possibility of error about the fundamental meanings and purposes of our moral practices. Such analysis dispels the alleged "permanence and continued justifiability" of our moral practices and the interpretations of those practices.

Part of the reason we are beguiled by the "permanence" of our moral interpretations of a practice is that we mistake an "outward" custom or way of doing things for a stability in *the meaning and purpose* of the practice. Again, Nietzsche has some insight to offer on this point in a discussion of the moral practice of punishment:

> One must distinguish two aspects: on the one hand, that in it which is relatively *enduring*, the custom, the act, the "drama," a certain strict sequence of procedures; on the other, that in it which is *fluid*, the meaning, the purpose, the expectation associated with the performance of such procedures. . . . [I]t is assumed without further ado that the procedure itself will be something older, earlier than its employment in punishment, that the latter is *projected* and interpreted *into* the procedure (which has existed but been employed in another sense), in short, that the case is not as has hitherto been assumed by our naive genealogists of law and morals, who have one

and all thought of the procedure as invented for the purpose of punishing, just as one formerly thought of the hand as invented for the purpose of grasping.[24]

Nietzsche argues that we are beguiled into ignoring the fluid meaning and purposes of a practice such as punishment when we focus too much on certain "external features" of the custom of punishing. We tend to read our own uses of the practice into the "nature" of the practice as such. Thus on the one hand we ignore divergent historical uses and meanings of the practice of punishment. On the other hand, when we do pay attention to history, we tend to view our current uses for a practice as a culmination of some necessary teleological progress. Genealogical analysis demonstrates that a moral practice at two different times appears superficially similar in terms of the explicit codes and rites of the practice. It appears that people have been punishing lawbreakers for a long time, but as Nietzsche argues, this practice is only superficially the same over time. It has served vastly different purposes, and indeed we might never be able to determine why we engage in the practice.[25] To take another example, Foucault argues that it *seems* that certain sexual taboos are the same over time (e.g., prohibitions against extramarital and same-sex relations). However, these taboos are different in salient respects. Taking one among many of the differences that Foucault analyzes, Greek sexual prohibitions were for the purpose of greater self-mastery, whereas for the Christians the goal was purification.[26]

Genealogy seems, then, to be concerned with correcting distortions in our moral interpretations. I have just been emphasizing the error of mistaking a current interpretation of the purpose of a prohibition with the meaning of the prohibition at all times. This is only part of the story. The problem may go beyond the fact that we have false beliefs about the *histories* of our values and the interpretations attached to them. We may also fail to understand the way our mores actually function *here and now.* *This* failure may result in various sorts of harm. In some instances, our flawed understandings may lead us to do the very thing that we thought our practice was designed to alleviate.[27]

An example will help. We might be mistaken in our current moral interpretation of the practice of institutionalizing the insane. We justify this practice by moral norms connected to "beneficence" (e.g., it is obligatory to set aside resources to help those who are ill and cannot help themselves, etc.). But assume that genealogical inquiry into the history of this practice shows that institutionalizing the insane does not, in any straightforward way, help alleviate insanity. We may notice that this practice is developed in tandem with a whole host of disciplining practices that come into play with the advent of various sorts of techniques and bodies of knowledge. This genealogy might call into question the notion that one could characterize the condition of "being insane" as some "natural" psychological disease of individuals. We may find that this "disease" is inextricably tied to a complex of historically contingent practices embedded in the very institutions (e.g., mental hospitals and clinics) that we thought were designed to alleviate insanity.[28]

GENEALOGY AND RADICAL MORAL SKEPTICISM

Even though we could be deeply wrong in our moral interpretations of what a practice actually does, we are not thereby committed to radical moral skepticism. After all, we might hold that norms of beneficence are still justified even though in *this* case, they are not appropriately realized by institutionalizing people. Genealogy helps to reveal how moral norms of beneficence are undermined in the way mental institutions actually function here and now. If we are committed to beneficence, we need to alter (perhaps completely) mental institutions and find other ways to deal with psychological problems.

Genealogy, in short, need not be put forth as a critique of fundamental moral norms. Rather, it may be viewed as a social critic's tool—useful for uncovering possible misinterpretations in our practices. The special difficulty with our moral interpretation of the norm of beneficence in this case is tied to the fact that the "outward customs" of this practice appear similar to acts of real beneficence. For example, administering therapy and drugs, keeping a vigilant meticulous watch over the patients, and so on all appear to be expressions of care and concern. In some respects, the activity of psychiatrists resembles other benevolent acts, say, that of a parent tending to the needs of a sick child. What genealogy shows us is that care of a mental patient is in fact quite different. The outwardly benevolent acts are masquerades beneath which something much more insidious occurs, namely the simultaneous production and control of the "mentally ill." Genealogical analysis is controversial in part because these acts function *like* what in other circumstances are clear instances of an acceptable moral norm. The "discipline," for example, that may be carried out though therapeutic techniques in the mental hospital is a "masked" discipline. It is not a clear violation of moral norms of beneficence or noninterference such as we see, for example, in a case of unprovoked physical assault.

The point to note in light of these remarks is that although genealogy helps to unmask our mistaken interpretations of moral norms, nothing said so far implies that practicing genealogy undermines morality as such. After all, at least part of what grounds the normative force of genealogical analysis in the example is that we are committed to norms of beneficence. If there is a skeptical stance in the understanding of genealogy given so far, it is a "local" skepticism. It is skepticism about the way in which moral norms function in some particular practice or institution. The example shows that the genealogical "unmasking" seems to make more straightforward sense in the light of commitment to some moral norms that the genealogist shows in a given instance to be undermined. It is interesting to note that if the results of genealogy appear scandalous, it is because norms we take for granted as governing moral practices are undermined by what we thought were exemplars of these norms. That is, the feeling of scandal can be explained by the belief in the value of some moral norm. Genealogical debunking would only be scandalous to those who either do not adequately understand it or who understand it but still have a hankering for a world view that they know to be false.

Even if radical moral skepticism is not a serious threat, is there another kind of skepticism lurking behind a hypercritical attitude that demands that we continuously give genealogies of our own genealogies? This worry could be put in formal and practical terms. On the formal side, one might hold that the genealogist falls prey to a kind of infinite regress. But a regress only follows if the genealogist accepts the principle that every genealogical inquiry requires a genealogy. I see no reason that the genealogist need accept this principle. To be sure, I see no way to offer in the abstract some set of conditions that require genealogical inquiry. But this seems to present no real problem. We do not expect the specification of such conditions in other areas of inquiry, so we should not expect it here. Secondly, the "formal" regress is blocked by virtue of the fact that a particular genealogy is aimed at clearing up incoherences in our understandings of particular practices and norms—not *every* norm-governed practice. The fact that genealogy puts some particular norm-governed practice in doubt does not imply that we must put every other set of normative commitments into doubt.

These points tie into the practical worry. It might be argued that the reflective stance fostered by genealogy leads to a kind of hyperreflexivity that results in paralysis and inaction. This worry has an epistemic and moral formulation. On the epistemic side, one might worry that genealogy fosters "doubt" about ever knowing whether a moral practice is justified or whether in fact it "masks" undesirable features. I think the worry is misplaced. To be sure, any genealogical analysis is subject to revision. However, decisions about what sorts of revisions in moral practices are appropriate and when we can bring self-interrogation to a provisional end can only be made in light of a detailed account of the particular practice and the context of its use.[29]

Foucault's own involvement with criticism of "mental hospitals" is instructive here. For a while, in Italy, mental patients were released from institutions. The results of this experiment were not particularly successful, as the patients ended up encountering all sorts of difficulties when left to themselves. This suggests that there is at least prima facie reason to doubt this particular criticism of mental hospitals. The Italian experiment is not sufficient reason to shed all suspicion about these medical practices. What it may point to is that if these practices require change, something less than complete abolition is in order.

The moral formulation of the indecisiveness objection maintains that the reflective attitude fostered by genealogy may tend to undermine confidence in morality. That is, assuming such a hypothetical, tentative stance toward moral norms and practices may lead people to be more willing to set aside moral considerations. I see no reason to believe that this projection is likely to be true. In fact, I would argue that the reflective, tentative attitude fostered by genealogy may be morally desirable on the grounds that honesty and self-reflexiveness are morally praiseworthy traits. Moreover, aside from the possible intrinsic moral value of the reflective attitudes fostered by genealogy, it seems plausible to hold that such attitudes have instrumental value insofar as they tend to enhance the quality of deliberation about moral problems. In short, the nondogmatic, fallibilistic stance taken by the genealogist may be valued for the same reasons we value such traits in other kinds of inquiry, namely, because they are crucial to the goal of generating and testing knowledge claims.

GENEALOGICAL INQUIRY
AND DETERMINATION PROBLEMS

Recall the model of deliberative events:

(1) There is an indeterminate situation, including a felt sense of trouble due to a failure of habits.

(2) There is a preliminary interpretation of the problem, including a view of what important goods and evils are at issue.

(3) Action plans are created that attempt to take account of the important goods and evils at issue.

(4) These action plans are tested in imaginative trials.

(5) The most promising plan is tested in actions bringing about change in the situation.

(6) These steps can be repeated by others or used to explain to others what was learned.

Determination problems involve warrant-establishing arguments that conclude with action plans, expressed in steps three and four. Genealogies of practices (and the interpretations we give of these), in the view defended here, concern steps 1 and 2. Often, the social critic offering a genealogy is working toward getting the community to see a practice or activity as a problem. Moreover, genealogies of practices and their interpretations will bear on several related deliberative events relating to these practices and activities. If you consider a problem such as the moral status of nonhuman animals, it should be clear that a genealogical analysis of our moral attitudes toward animals will be applicable to a range of deliberative events involving the treatment of animals in farming, scientific experiments, and hunting (among others). Therefore, strictly speaking, genealogical interpretation furnishes fresh perspectives that apply to steps 1 and 2 in a range of related deliberative events.

It should be no surprise that social critics provoke us to view our norm-governed practices in a different light. Remember that habits or norms are ways of thinking, feeling, and doing. They structure our interpretations of our world. It is often difficult to step back from them and question some of the tacit assumptions built into them. Although social critics can help in the project of such critical inquiry, actual transformation of habits is a more involved matter requiring change in conditions as much as attitudes. Changing deep-seated attitudes about the moral acceptability of meat diets may require encounters with slaughterhouses (in order to see the actual context of this habit) and vegetarian cooking (in order to see alternative habits) as much as encounters with social critics who explore the interpretive assumptions behind these practices.

THE CASE OF CHARITY

In her book *Democracy and Social Ethics,* Jane Addams gives an insightful analysis of the problems confronting "charity workers" (the late-nineteenth-century equivalent of what we today call social workers).[30] Addams points out that the norm of charity is problematic in the context of middle-class individuals whose vocation is to minister to the poor. Those ministered to are suspicious of the charity given. Addams locates a variety of explanations for such suspicion. One explanation is the fact that the charity is provided within the confines of a nine-to-five job, rather than being given spontaneously whenever needed. Connected to this point is the widespread belief that the motivation for work is to be (as it was put at the time) "on the make," that is, trying to gain as much money as possible with little if any regard for the well-being of others. Another reason for the suspicion of charity workers given by Addams is the fact that a whole administrative apparatus was brought to bear on the charity recipients. Thus charity workers do not simply minister to the needs of the poor, they also monitor their progress, use expert knowledge to offer advice and so on. In short, the "charity" delivered by the charity workers is their job, not the result of spontaneous good will or friendship.

Addams quite consciously attempts to understand charity as a historical entity whose character is shaped by concrete social practices. She is aware that the suspicions surrounding charity come from the social positions occupied by the giver and the recipient. She relates these social positions to an account of the industrial system of her time, which was the very source of widespread and concentrated urban poverty as well as certain views about work and morality. Granted, Addams' genealogy of the charity norm does not attempt to give a comprehensive history of this norm and the way in which it functions in all social contexts. However, such a sweeping genealogy would not be to the point of the problems that she addresses. But she does try to bring out the fact that charity functions differently in industrial society than it functioned in prior social arrangements. In fact, charity functions differently within industrial society depending on who provides it (e.g., one's working-class neighbors or the charity worker). We can also see in this example that the moral interpretations of both charity workers and the poor are not completely in error. Both parties are somewhat aware that the charity provided is suspect. What it took to explicitly bring out the nature of these problematic interpretations was someone like Addams who was both intimately involved with this type of charity work and yet reflective enough about the larger historical and social context in which this work was carried out.

It might be asked, What in this example would be the point of interrogating the moral interpretations of charity? Here are a few thoughts. Explicitly recognizing that the administration of charity is implicated in these larger, usually unacknowledged social relations and conditions is a first step toward developing a realistic assessment not only of the relations between particular charity workers and particular poor people but also of the larger social problems that create this sort of social relationship. Recognizing these larger social problems might be a first step in gaining needed trust between individuals in different social strata. That, in turn, might help form a concerted social response to these larger problems, which will no doubt lead to the adjudication of other problematic moral norms (perhaps connected to work, the family, and politics). The bottom line is that a genealogical "stepping back" from our immediate moral interpretations in order to correct them in light of understanding the larger sociohistorical context in which they function might often be a valuable precursor to dealing more reflectively and honestly with a variety of deliberative events treating moral problems relating to class divisions. Thus, genealogy can be thought of as a sometimes useful tool for the project of forging publics (in the Deweyan sense of that term). Genealogical inquiry can be thought of as a contribution to the practice of social criticism understood as immanent critique.

THE CASE OF ANIMALS

In the past three decades philosophers like Peter Singer and Tom Regan have applied standard moral theories to nonhuman animals. Singer shows how, among other things, a utilitarian concern for alleviating the unnecessary suffering of any sentient beings throws factory farming and the meat diets this practice supports into moral doubt.[31] Regan argues that any adequate theory of individual rights must conclude that those animals that are what he calls "subjects-of-a-life" should not be used as means for human ends.[32] The rights view would call for an absolute abolition of practices like hunting and research. Philosophers like Regan and Singer have had a real impact on social movements for animal liberation. Here we have a compelling example of how contemporary moral philosophers use their theoretical perspectives to criticize practices and organize social groups. What is interesting, from a pragmatist perspective, is that the effectiveness of the social criticism may be not so much a matter of converting citizens to adopt utilitarian or rights moral theories, but rather of how these philosophers recontextualize the practices involving animals by interpreting familiar moral principles in a new light. But even more to our point here, some animal rights philosophers supplement their normative arguments with detailed genealogies of our moral attitudes toward animals and the practices within which these attitudes function. These genealogical interpretations do not necessarily presuppose adopting a particular moral theory. Consider the following.

In the West, many of the assumptions about animals come from the Judeo-Christian and Greek traditions of thought. According to Christians, humans are made in God's image, endowed with souls. Animals are different in kind from humans—soulless beings placed on earth by God for human benefit. According to much Greek philosophy, humans are different from animals by virtue of the fact that we have rational souls. It is not morally wrong for rational beings to use nonrational beings for their purposes because, somehow, rationality has the only ultimate value.[33]

Now, if Darwin's theory of evolution is correct, it is no longer plausible to view human beings as different in kind from nonhuman animals. Humans lie on a continuum with other nonhuman animals. By virtue of this fact, it is entirely plausible to attribute capacities such as emotions, feelings, and even some level of reasoning to many nonhuman animals. It is no longer plausible, after Darwin, to think that these capacities are the special province of the human species. At the very least, then, the "image of God" thesis is challenged by Darwin. If it is no longer plausible to view animals as different in kind from humans, then it is at least less plausible to believe that their interests can simply be dismissed. The same would seem to hold true of the rationality thesis. Some animals have at least a degree of the rationality that humans do. Moreover, some humans have less rationality than some nonhuman animals. Therefore, it is not at all obvious how "rationality" may function as a neat moral dividing line between humans and nonhumans.[34]

Consider the scientific practice of using animals in experiments. Historically, scientists have assumed that animals do not feel pain, or that their pain is insignificant. One common reason for this belief is the notion that pain states are not properly verifiable. This in turn is tied to a certain kind of verificationist view of scientific method that has been much criticized. Another factor in the scientific dismissal of animal suffering is the view that in some sense science is a "value-free" enterprise, which need not concern itself with moral questions about animals. This view of science may be tied as much to verificationist or behaviorist ideology, which claims that values are not measurable and thus are not the concern of the scientists. Or they may also be tied to a kind of narrow professionalism that shields science from scrutiny in order to protect the career status of its participants. A genealogical study of the sort offered by Bernard Rollin may enable us to trace the development of these ideas about science as well as the institutional context of science. What is especially striking, as Rollin notes, is the way that twentieth-century science ignores the very implications that Darwinian theory has for taking seriously the consciousness and pain of nonanimal human animals.[35] In some sense, many scientific research practices are at odds with some of its central theoretical assumptions about evolutionary biology.

These brief remarks about the philosophical treatment of ethics and animals demonstrate the ways in which philosophers challenge uncritical assumptions by situating our prereflective attitudes toward animals in a larger context of practices with histories. Even nonpragmatist philosophers can commit to the pragmatist model of deliberative events, including most especially the importance of clarifying the preliminary interpretation of a problem by recontextualzing our ordinary understandings. The pragmatist view seems enough of an all-purpose theoretical tool to be of use to philosophers who may disagree about other theoretical matters.

Conclusion

Conclusions of philosophy books often contain a humble acknowledgment that says something such as "I wish I could say there was nothing false in these pages, but . . ." As a pragmatist, I would rather put the sentiment this way: "I don't expect that everything I could say in this book is the final truth about morality, and I fully expect that whatever truths are in it need further development in cooperation with others." No book can be the last word on a subject like "morality." If my claims in this book are on the right track, then other inquiries would certainly be necessary. These would include further research in social theory and moral psychology. If moral considerations are habits, then study of the actual structure of the mind is a central part of a full theory of morality. If moral considerations are *socially shared* habits, then social theory is a part of moral theory. Furthermore, as I mentioned at the end of Chapter 2, a complete pragmatist value theory needs further development and defense.

At the very least, I hope that I have shown the significance of the hypothesis that morality is comprised of "norms" or "habits" for topics such as the theory of practical reason, moral epistemology, moral argument, and social criticism. Perhaps at another level, the significance of this pragmatist hypothesis may be that it helps us to make sense of the contingency of morality, without reducing morality to arbitrary convention, or subjective "emoting." I find that adopting this hypothesis provides a way of appreciating our moral convictions and commitments with a certain degree of humility. As individuals we are brief carriers of the disparate moral habits that define our responsibilities for social relationships. These relationships express a plethora of contingent values. We find ourselves responsible for these contingent relationships and practices. With the dawning of our recognition of this responsibility comes the recognition of the need to make rational sense of our moral habits. At the very least, pragmatist philosophy can help us combine the twin aims of any rational ethics: commitment to those social practices and relationships that represent fundamental values, and commitment to criticism of these practices so that we can learn together how to make them better.

Embracing this hypothesis about the contingent roots of morality might seem to lead to a pessimistic demotion of our moral commitments. After all, if morality is nothing more than learned habits geared toward contingent, transitory projects, why give in to its "demands"? What does it matter from the point of view of the universe? From the point of view of the universe, it may not matter much. We may gain special insights from efforts to take a perspective that makes our practices and lives look small. In fact, from a distance such views might actually help us to appreciate certain kinds of values by widening our vision beyond those cares and concerns that attach to our own personal fates. Such a point of view—what Santayana calls "the realm of spirit"—merits exploration into areas beyond the subject matter explored in this book. But before we pursue such views from a distance, we should not forget the other perspectives that define us in our concrete connection to contingent activities and practices. There is no reason we cannot appreciate our responsibilities for, and commitments to, these practices in light of a frankly secular acknowledgment of their transiency.

Notes

Introduction

1. In this book I will frequently talk about what "pragmatists" believe. I make no pretense that there is some kind of universal consensus among pragmatists about how to approach morality. Many pragmatists will have different ideas about what is most important in a pragmatist ethics.

2. Among the classical pragmatists, Dewey is the clearest about this radical reconstruction of the notion of theory. I think that among Dewey interpreter Michael Eldridge has done the best job in demonstrating that the notion of "intelligent practice" best captures what is central in Dewey's pragmatic philosophy. See his *Transforming Experience: John Dewey's Cultural Instrumentalism* (Nashville: Vanderbilt University Press, 1998).

3. Dewey offers just this sort of psychological explanation for this kind of idealization. See especially *The Quest For Certainty,* vol. 4 of *The Later Works, 1925–1953* [hereinafter cited as *LW*], ed. Jo Ann Boydston (Carbondale: Southern Illinois University Press; London: Feffer & Simons, 1981–1990), and *Experience and Nature,* vol. 1 of *LW.*

4. It is worth noting that pragmatists bear a certain affinity to the Hegelian tradition, including the Marxist offshoot of that tradition. Like Hegel and Marx, pragmatists seek to locate human rationality and human morality inside historically contingent practices. Though pragmatists such as Dewey reject the idea that there is a discernible pattern of development in human practices like that found in Hegelian absolute idealism and Marxist historical materialism, pragmatists, Hegelians, and Marxists are allies in their attempt to make philosophy "concrete" by identifying philosophical concepts in social prac-

tices. This very attempt to restore concreteness to philosophy is as a contribution to our attempts to use reason to arrive at an accurate, honest understanding of what it is to be rational in thought and action. Pragmatists, Hegelians, and Marxists are engaging in "self-critique." Making philosophy more concrete is not using philosophy to satisfy narrow wants or desires. It is the pursuit of a more honest self-understanding. At the least, such honesty will help us pursue practices with integrity and wisdom, making the most of these practices in the brief time that we have to use them.

5. *LW* 1:34.
6. Ibid. 7:163.
7. Ibid., 164.
8. Ibid., 165.
9. These pragmatist efforts are well under way. See, for example, Andrew Light and Eric Katz, eds., *Environmental Pragmatism* (London: Routledge, 1996), and Glen McGee, *The Perfect Baby: A Pragmatic Approach to Genetics* (Lanham, Md.: Rowman and Littlefied, 1997).
10. "Pragmatic Ethics," in *The Blackwell Guide to Ethical Theory,* ed. Hugh LaFollette (Malden: Blackwell, 2000), 400.
11. *Ethics: Inventing Right and Wrong* (Harmondsworth, N.Y.: Penguin, 1977).
12. *After Virtue,* 2nd ed. (Notre Dame: University of Notre Dame Press, 1984).
13. Ithaca: Cornell University Press, 1995.
14. In *Reading Dewey: Interpretations for a Postmodern Generation,* ed. Larry A. Hickman (Bloomington: Indiana University Press, 1998).
15. Set out in *Beyond Deduction: Ampliative Aspects of Philosophical Reflection* (New York: Routledge, 1988).
16. Ithaca: Cornell University Press, 1988.
17. Ithaca: Cornell University Press, 1996.
18 In *The Blackwell Guide,* 400–420.

Chapter 1

1. A useful discussion of the idea of "ideal" versus "minimal" rationality can be found in Thomas M. Scanlon, *What We Owe to Each Other* (Cambridge: Belknap Press of Harvard University Press, 1998), 30–36.
2. A popular account is that intentional explanation must make reference to desires (or some kind of pro-attitude) and beliefs, both of

which figure in a reason that is taken to be a proximate cause of an action. See for example Donald Davidson's "Actions, Reasons, and Causes," in *Essays on Actions and Events* (New York: Oxford University Press, 1980).

3. A good sample of the debate here can be found in Samuel Scheffler, ed., *Consequentialism and Its Critics,* (New York: Oxford University Press, 1988). See also Thomas Nagel's *The View from Nowhere* (New York: Oxford University Press, 1986), 152–88.

4. We can set aside the question of how to treat cases in which a person is deceived about the nature of her own intentions. It is possible that in pathological cases our third-party explanations will show how someone has an incomplete or (more radically) a completely false understanding of her intentions.

5. *Nicomachean Ethics,* trans. Terence Irwin (Indianapolis: Hackett Books, 1985) 1094a20-21, p. 2.

6. *An Enquiry Concerning the Principles of Morals,* ed. J. B. Shneewind (Indianapolis: Hackett, 1983), 87.

7. John Stuart Mill offers another argument in *Utilitarianism* (Indianapolis: Hackett, 1986), 2:

> All action is for the sake of some end, and rules of action, it seems natural to suppose, must take their whole character and color from the end to which they are subservient. When we engage in pursuit, a clear and precise conception of what we are pursuing would seem to be the first thing we need, instead of the last we are to look forward to. A test of right and wrong must be the means, one would think, of ascertaining what is right and wrong, and not a consequence of having already ascertained it.

Mill says that practical arts require some conception of the end they serve before they can be applied because we need a test of right and wrong antecedent to our deliberations about action. The general end thus serves as a "test" or means for evaluation.

8. The Dreyfuses develop a five-stage sequence of skill acquisition. Of the novice stage, they write, "Normally, the instruction process begins with the instructor decomposing the task environment into context-free features which the beginner can recognize without the benefit of experience. The beginner is then given rules for determining actions on the basis of these features, like following a com-

puter program." Hubert I. Dreyfus and Stuart E. Dreyfus, "What Is Morality?: A Phenomenological Account of the Development of Ethical Expertise," in *Universalism versus Communitarianism,* ed. D. Rasmussen (Cambridge: MIT Press, 1990), 240.

9. My idea here is similar to what John Searle means by the "background." For Searle, the background is a network of nonrepresentational assumptions required to make sense of the representative character of any intentional act. See his *Intentionality: An Essay in the Philosophy of Mind* (New York: Cambridge University Press, 1983). Mark Johnson makes similar claims in the chapter entitled "The Narrative Context of Self and Action" in his *Moral Imagination: Implications of Cognitive Science for Ethics* (Chicago: The University of Chicago Press, 1993), 150-84.

10. See *Beyond Deduction,* 147–48.

11. "The Rational Governance of Practice," in *Pragmatism and Realism,* ed. Kenneth Westphal, (Lanham, Md.: Rowman and Littlefield, 1997), 69–70.

12. *The Middle Works: 1899–1924,* ed. Jo Ann Boydston, vol. 14 (Carbondale: Southern Illinois University Press, 1976–1983) [Hereinafter cited as *MW*], 15.

13. Pierre Bourdieu's account of what he calls the habitus is a social scientific notion that is very close to the view Deweyan view of habits as culturally acquired patterns of perception and behavior, especially the notion that practical knowledge is the product of patterned ways of dealing with situations. Bourdieu's focus is the way in which class structures condition these habitus structures. The latter in turn condition perceptions of social reality. Bourdieu downplays the possibility of reflective understanding of these structures and accordingly the possibility of rationally modifying these. For a good graphic representation of the habitus model, see *Distinction: A Social Critique of the Judgment of Taste,* translated by Richard Nice, (Cambridge: Harvard University Press, 1984), 171. See also *Outline of a Theory of Practice,* trans. Richard Nice (Cambridge: Cambridge University Press, 1977).

14. "The Rational Governance of Practice," 68–69.

15. As Dewey puts it, habits have a "beginning, middle and end. Each stage marks progress in dealing with materials and tools, advance in converting material to active use." *MW* 14:16.

16. *MW* 14:19.

17. Will makes a similar point about the possibility of creative individual transformation of a community's standards through the use of those

very standards: "Each individual is a vessel, holding, expressing, utilizing, and often altering in use some portion of the entire corpus of communal practices. That any one of us may develop and commit ourselves to standards which diverge from those of the communities which formed us is misunderstood by some as evidence that there is in us a capacity to discern standards that is quite independent of communities" (*Beyond Deduction*, 90).

18. James D. Wallace makes the point that understanding history is important for understanding virtually any domain of practical knowledge. See his *Ethical Norms, Particular Cases*, 9–12.

19. I have in mind here views such as what Bernard Williams calls "Government House utilitarianism." Some utilitarians hold that we might have good utilitarian reasons for not using the principle of utility in our deliberations about what we ought to do. Utilitarian policy makers might, for example, advocate publicly that people follow "esoteric" morality because privately they believe this is best way to maximize utility. See his *Ethics and the Limits of Philosophy* (Cambridge: Harvard University Press, 1985), 108–10.

20. *Twenty Years at Hull House*, ed. James Hurt (Urbana: University of Illinois Press, 1990), 42.

21. *Hull House*, 45. The point that Addams makes about "deferred purpose" at the end of this quote links up with the title of the chapter, "The Snare of Preparation" (a phrase Addams borrows from Tolstoy). One can be caught in the snare of preparation to the extent that one suspends making a choice because of a vague sense that the opportunity for action waits in some distant future.

22. *Hull House*, 43.

23. Ibid., 42.

24. Ibid., 52.

25. To reiterate, the "end" or "practical reason" that plays the justificatory role could be understood in a variety of ways by a variety of theories. Bernard Williams would hold that all ends that guide conduct by giving reasons for action are "internal" in the sense that they "display a relativity of the reason statement to the agent's *subjective motivational set.*" Basically Williams argues that if it is true that a reason is a reason for a person, then that reason must have some support in the person's existing motivations. Addams must have some desires or interests in her motivational set—such as the desire to do socially useful work—relative to which she has a reason to found a settlement house. The external reasons theorist, on the other

hand, would claim that reasons might exist for actions that do not display such relativity to motivational sets. Such reasons, if they exist, are reasons for a person to perform some action even in the absence of any desire, inclination, or interest to take the action. So if Addams has an external reason to found a settlement house, then she has this reason even if she had absolutely no desire to do anything but pursue a career as a physician and spend her summers on tour in Europe (obviously, there is no lack of motivation in this example). See Williams' *Moral Luck: Philosophical Papers, 1973–1980* (New York: Cambridge University Press, 1981), 102.

26. This schema mirrors what Dewey calls the pattern of inquiry. See his *Logic: The Theory of Inquiry,* in *LW,* vol. 12.

27. I do not want to argue that every time a person deliberates, she must represent the event in precisely the way that I set out above. The important point is that the basic features of the deliberative event are somehow represented by the person.

28. Hugh LaFollette uses the phrase "second-order habits" in "Pragmatic Ethics."

29. *Hull House,* 43–44.

30. Ibid., 66 (my emphasis).

31. "Pragmatism, Davidson, and Truth," in *Objectivity, Relativism, and Truth* (Cambridge: Cambridge University Press, 1991), 128.

32. I have been influenced by Hilary and Ruth Ann Putnam's account of Dewey's view of changes in ends, especially in connection to "inquiry." See their "Dewey's Logic" in *Words and Life,* ed. James Conant (Cambridge: Harvard University Press, 1994).

33. One might argue that these ultimate justificatory ends are known by a kind of noninferential intuition. I take it that appeals to intuition do not help explain what one learns when one sees that a new end is needed. One need only see this by reflecting on the fact that such appeals reveal absolutely nothing to others about why one's mind has changed.

34. A recent example is Henry Richardson, "Truth and Ends in Dewey's Pragmatism," in *Pragmatism ,* vol. 24 of *Canadian Journal of Philosophy,* ed. Cheryl Misak (Calgary: University of Calgary Press, 1999).

35. I think that it makes little difference whether we say that Addams had two closely related problems or that one very complex problem with two interrelated aspects, the suffering of the poor and her sense of implication in that suffering on the one hand and deep-seated early-childhood psychoses on the other.

36. James Tiles, "Rationality Beyond Deduction," in *Pragmatism, Reason, and Norms: A Realistic Assessment,* ed. Kenneth R. Westphal (New York: Fordham University Press, 1998), 287.

37. *MW* 14:21.

38. Ibid., 24.

39. Ibid., 25.

40. Ibid., 32.

Chapter 2

1. Arthur Edward Murphy, *The Theory of Practical Reason,* ed. A. I. Melden (La Salle, Ill.: Open Court Publishing, 1964), 57–80.

2. *What We Owe to Each Other,* 96–100.

3. Ibid., 97.

4. See *Principia Ethica,* Chapter 1 (Cambridge: Cambridge University Press, 1993).

5. *What We Owe to Each Other,* 96–97.

6. Basically, I agree with Scanlon's way of putting this point: "goodness and value . . . (are) non-natural properties, namely the purely formal, higher-order properties that provide reasons of the relevant kind," (*What We Owe to Each Other,* 97). I would ask why we ought to call this formal higher order property nonnatural. Action plans and the judgments they embed are not qualities of objects like "red" or "large." However, they are qualities of behavior that seem observable.

7. *After Virtue,* 189.

8. Ibid., 188.

9. *LW* 1:274–75.

10. Scanlon makes a related point. See *What We Owe to Each Other,* 88–89.

11. *Moral Relevance and Moral Conflict,* 96–133.

12. Ibid., 117.

13. Perhaps it is plausible to assume that when the pursuit of some activity impinges (indirectly) on other areas of human good, some means other than "self-regulation" must be implemented. Dewey accounts for the notion of a "public" in terms of those who are so affected by the activities of private parties. The representatives of a public are part of the "state."

14. *Nicomachean Ethics,* 1106a33, p. 43.

15. *MW* 14:146–47.
16. Frederick Will, "Philosophic Governance of Norms," in *Pragmatism and Realism,* ed. Kenneth R. Westphal (Lanham, Md.: Rowman and Littlefield, 1997), 166.
17. This seems to be Dewey's view. See, for example, *MW* 14:202–3.

Chapter 3

1. *MW* 14:216–17.
2. Dewey no doubt is influenced here by Hume's moral philosophy. Hume takes judgments of approbation about character as his starting point in *An Enquiry Concerning the Principles of Morals.*
3. However, as I shall argue shortly, the idea that there are two steps here is questionable.
4. *Constructions of Reason* (New York: Cambridge University Press, 1989), 181.
5. Ibid., 181.
6. Kant discusses these maxims in section 40 of *Critique of Judgment,* trans. Werner S. Pluhar (Indianapolis: Hackett, 1988; originally published in 1790).
7. I believe that a similar problem exists in Jürgen Habermas' discourse ethics. Habermas makes a strict separation between the justification of norms and their application to particular cases. In some respects, Habermas' account of "discourse" and "communicative action" has much in common with the pragmatist account of deliberative events that I develop in this book. See his *Moral Consciousness and Communicative Action,* trans. Christian Lenhardt and Shierry Weber Nicholsen (Cambridge: MIT Press, 1990), and *Justification and Application: Remarks on Discourse Ethics,* trans. Ciaran P. Cronin (Cambridge: MIT Press, 1993).
8. This view, by the way, fits nicely with noncognitivist accounts of moral judgment. In these views we can always break a moral conviction down into two easily separable components: pro-attitudes and beliefs. See John McDowell, "Non-Cognitivism and Rule-Following," in *Wittgenstein: To Follow a Rule,* ed. Steven H. Holtzman and Christopher M. Leich (London: Routledge and Kegan Paul, 1981). McDowell does a good job of demonstrating precisely how noncognitivism flows from assuming that we can peel off the cognitive and noncognitive components and view the latter from a standpoint "external" to the moral outlook of a person.

9. "Education as Norm Acquisition," in Westphal, *Pragmatism, Reason, and Norms: A Realistic Assessment,* 167.

10. In *Mind* 92 (1983): 530–47.

11. Ibid., 546.

12. Ibid., 533.

13. I develop the claim that moral principles are an aspect of moral norms later in the chapter.

14. Pragmatism takes moral reasoning to be a process of squaring particular judgments with principles. This is somewhat like what John Rawls calls "reflective equilibrium." The difference here, briefly, is that Rawls seems to regard reflective equilibrium as a process for arriving at an adequate description of the original position and the justice principles that would be chosen there. The pragmatist view of moral judgment that I defend squares generals and particulars for the purpose of arriving at an adequate action plan to solve particular problems. See Rawls, *A Theory of Justice* (Cambridge: Belknap Press of Harvard University Press, 1971), 47–50.

15. See "Ethical Particularism," 538.

16. *The Abuse of Casuistry: A History of Moral Reasoning* (Berkeley: University of California Press, 1988), 18–19.

17. "Getting Down to Cases: The Revival of Casuistry in Bioethics," *Journal of Medicine and Philosophy* 16 (1991): 29–51.

18. *The Abuse of Casuistry,* 67–68.

19. Ibid., 89.

20. *Freedom and Reason* (New York: Oxford University Press, 1963), 37–42.

21. *The Abuse of Casuistry,* 257.

22. Ibid., 258 (my emphasis).

23. Ibid., 39–40.

24. The routine use of norms may be reflective or unreflective. We speak of "moral judgments" in unreflective instances of moral life in the same way we speak of a person who is a good judge of prize dogs in that she can readily (without much reflection) pick out the quality dogs from others. Of course in these cases the unreflective judgment is the refined product of prior practice and perhaps even prior explicit deliberation.

25. An illuminating discussion of these and other aspects of moral habits can be found in LaFollette's "Pragmatic Ethics," especially pp. 406–8. It seems to me that Aristotle and the virtue ethics tradition explore the habitual dimension of moral life with great care. The

virtuous person has a habit of acting in the right way and feeling the correct emotions, given the appropriate circumstances. Nevertheless, to speak of a "moral expert" should not mislead us into thinking either that expertise is ever fixed once and for all or that a person is an expert in all areas of moral life. The idea that moral personality is multifaceted, along with an argument rejecting the ancient notion that "virtue is one," can be found in Owen Flanagan's *Varieties of Moral Personality: Ethics and Psychological Realism* (Cambridge: Harvard University Press, 1991).

26. For a good discussion of the "clustering" of moral norms see James D. Wallace, *Ethical Norms, Particular Cases,* 23–39.

27. Dewey and James H. Tufts, *Ethics, LW* 7:280.

28. See *The Right and the Good* (Oxford: Clarendon Press, 1930).

29. *Ethical Norms, Particular Cases,* 22.

30. My suggestion to treat moral principles not as obligations to perform some act but rather as obligations to consider certain features of a situation or action is, of course, a "theoretical" revision of the phrase "moral principle," not meant necessarily to capture the ordinary understanding of this phrase. To some extent, pragmatist ethics is revisionist. However, to a quite different extent, pragmatist ethics is consistent with some of what we already do in everyday moral practice. The hope is that people can recognize their ordinary moral practice in the pragmatic account of moral principles. People should be able to see that we do confront hard cases in which goodwilled people disagree about what is proper. We see that in these hard cases, there is a place for reasoned argument, where "argument" has an educational function of discovering together what is important. When we give moral reasons in arguments about hard cases we are, by definition of the case, not simply trying to get other people to share our judgments about what to do. Rather, we are trying to find out with other, perhaps differently minded people what we ought to do in this case. After we have settled upon a solution of a moral problem, we may view moral reasons and arguments as simply conveying information about our settled convictions.

31. Toulmin, Stephen, *The Uses of Argument* (Cambridge: Cambridge University Press, 1958; reprint 1964). Most of my discussion is based on Chapter 3 of this work, "The Layout of Arguments."

32. "The Revival of Casuistry in Bioethics," 47.

33. *Case Studies in Medical Ethics* (Cambridge: Harvard University Press, 1977), 33–34.

34. Ibid., 18–19.
35. Ibid., 20.
36. Ibid., 20.
37. Ibid., 20.

Chapter 4

1. One could substitute "obligation" for "responsibility" without loss of meaning.

2. This account of responsibilities does not rule out, by definition, so called imperfect duties—those duties that allow the agent to choose who will be the recipients of the responsibility or obligation. For example, one might say that we have a standing duty to give to charity, but allow leeway about who the recipient may be. The recipient need not be a determinate individual or group. It may be that any person (agent) has a responsibility to give (value) to some needy people (recipient), yet it may still be a matter of free choice for the agent to determine who in the relevant class of recipients is chosen. I thank Hugh LaFollette for bringing this issue to my attention.

3. I am indebted to Claudia Card's account of moral responsibility. See her *The Unnatural Lottery: Character and Moral Luck* (Philadelphia: Temple University Press, 1996), 28. Also see Annette Baier's *Moral Prejudices: Essays on Ethics* (Cambridge: Harvard University Press, 1994).

4. For a good discussion of this debate from a defender of a social definition, see W. K. Frankena, "The Concept of Morality," in *The Definition of Morality*, ed. Gerald Wallace and A. D. M. Walker, (London: Methuen and Co., 1970), 146–73.

5. See Neil Cooper, "Morality and Importance," in Wallace and Walker, *The Definition of Morality*, 97.

6. Yet we must be careful here. Even a monk's pursuit of religious perfection in a monastery involves interactions with fellow monks. The point is that the object or aim of the monk's practice is a value that concerns his own personal salvation, just as the object or aim of an artist might be the development of his own artistic abilities.

7. For a statement of what it means to say that norms are unstructured, see Wallace, *Ethical Norms, Particular Cases,* 37–39.

8. *Ethical Norms, Particular Cases,* 38. In another discussion Wallace adds that it is futile to think that "living" is the activity that structures

moral norms because "living" really consists, for the most part, of
activities such as inquiry, family, healing, and so forth. See *Ethical
Norms, Particular Cases,* 14

9. See *MW* 14:220.

10. See *An Enquiry Concerning the Principles of Morals,* especially 48–51.

11. *MW* 14:57–58.

12. *LW* 7:217.

13. Dewey argues that although we can talk about "right" independently
of private desire, we should not cut moral rightness off from desire
as such (as Kantian theories tend to do with their bifurcation between empirical desire and the rational will). Moral norms regulate, and partly constitute, relationships.

14. *LW* 7:218.

15. Ibid., 227–28.

16. Ibid., 228. Dewey's theory of obligation draws on the Roman idea
that duties attach to *offices.* I prefer to speak of obligations as responsibilities for relationships, where the subjects and objects of responsibilities can range wider than defined roles or officeholders.
We simply need to keep this in mind, as we follow Dewey's discussion of "offices." As an officeholder, I am representative of a role. I
may violate my representative role when I abuse the office. Fla-
grant abuses would count as one kind of decision problem.

17. Ronald Dworkin develops a theory of legal interpretation that maintains that when people adopt an interpretive attitude towards some
practice that is in dispute they appropriately appeal to an interpretation of that practice in its "best light"—in the light of what purposes or ends the practice is designed to serve. See his *Law's Empire*
(Cambridge: Belknap Press of Harvard University Press, 1986), 50.

18. *LW* 7:231–32.

19. This point about the growth of "generalized sense of duty" can also
help to defeat the force of another related objection, namely, that
moral norms seem to apply to "humanity as such" but not to human beings in particular roles or relationships. The pragmatist can
consistently maintain that when the relations between human beings are tenuous or just forming (e.g., when two cultures first encounter one another) the moral norms appropriate for governing
the relations will be abstract and general. They will be those minimal norms that humans need to abide by if they are even to begin
to enter relations with each other. Perhaps the cultures only want
to go about their business without interfering with each other. If

this is so, then the norms regulating their interactions will be norms such as "do not kill," "do not harm," "do not restrict the autonomy of other human beings," and the like. But of course, in most cases of first cultural contact, what we have are the beginnings of a whole host of economic, cultural, social, and political relations. As these grow and develop, so too will norms whose authority will flow from their capacity to sustain and enhance these relationships.

20. *LW* 7:232–33.

21. For the pragmatist, the obligations embedded in social roles are not taken as inflexible codes of conduct but as resources for the adjudication of novel determination problems that may require change in the roles themselves. This fact separates pragmatism's use of "relationships" from that of a Hegelian like Bradley. Bradley believes that any analysis of "my station and its duties" cannot provide an understanding of what ought to be done in problematic cases. Bradley believes that no moral philosophy can be what he calls a "science" of moral prescriptions. Moral prescriptions—even in conflict cases—are arrived at through intuitive judgment. Perhaps Bradley takes such a dim view of rational reflection about duties because he believes that in some way the objective moral order reflects a kind of social mind that operates "behind the backs" of "individuals." See his "My Station and Its Duties," in *Ethical Studies*, 2nd ed. (New York: Oxford University Press, 1962), especially 193–95.

22. Mead makes some important remarks that tie into the connection between individuality and social roles. He claims that there is a sphere of concern and satisfaction connected to one's "function," the excellent exercise of which may result in a kind of "pride" that is not tied to any sort of hedonistic egoism. Moreover, the pride that one can justifiably take in one's function may be based on the fact that one may contribute to the transformation of the said function. Mead writes:

> One is a good surgeon, a good lawyer, and he can pride himself on his superiority–but it is a superiority which he makes use of. And when he does actually make use of it in the very community to which he belongs it loses that element of egoism which we think of when we think of a person simply pluming himself on his superiority over somebody else. . . . [W]hen the sense of superiority goes over into a functional expression, then it becomes not only entirely legitimate, but it is the way in which

individuals do change the situations in which they live. We change things by the capacities which we have that other people do not have.

Mead goes on to claim that exercising our abilities in some function in a way that others cannot, gives us a sense of superiority. The statement that "when the sense of superiority goes over into a functional expression, then it becomes entirely legitimate" may be a little incautious. Mead's basic point seems to be that an individual can realize himself by being able to exercise his capacities in a unique way, in specific role-related activities and practices. He writes, "It is only the ultimate effect that we can recognize, but the differences are due to the gestures of these countless individuals actually changing the situation in which they find themselves, although the specific changes are too minute for us to identify." *Mind, Self, and Society* (Lanham, Md.: Rowman and Littlefield, 1997), 203.

23. *LW* 7:231.
24. Hugh LaFollette uses the notion of moral niches in his "Pragmatic Ethics."

Chapter 5

1. No doubt philosophers may play the role of social critics, evaluating specific moral problems and offering possible solutions. However, that role may also be played by journalists, ministers, poets, scientists, or ordinary citizens.
2. Richard Rorty makes a related point when he writes "the poet and the revolutionary are protesting in the name of society itself against those aspects of the society that are unfaithful to its own self-image." *Contingency, Irony, and Solidarity* (Cambridge: Cambridge University Press, 1989), 60. Rorty's idea that "liberalism" need not defend its values by appeal to community-independent standards but rather by appeal to a sense of solidarity to a contingent community is close to the view that I defend in this book. I do think, however, that there is a place for relative detachment from particular communities. I am unsure to what extent Rorty would agree with me.
3. Michael, Walzer, *Interpretation and Social Criticism* (Cambridge: Harvard University Press, 1987), 40.
4. Ibid., 35.
5. Ibid., 64.

6. I take it that the extent to which this claim is defensible is a matter to be settled empirically—a matter I will not settle here.

7. Donald Davidson argues that when we interpret another's foreign language we must develop a theory of the meaning of that language on the basis of a principle of charity. This means that we assume agreement on a large portion of beliefs. This does not mean complete agreement will emerge. It does mean that for a meaningful discussion even to begin we must work from areas of agreement. We might apply the point to this case of social criticism. If I am a critic, I had better at least come to some initial agreement with my audience about basic normative or value conceptions if my ultimate aim is to convince them of some normative claim. See Davidson's "On the Very Idea of a Conceptual Scheme," in *Inquiries into Truth and Interpretation* (Oxford: Oxford University Press, 1984).

8. *LW* 2:245–46.

9. I will not elaborate on Dewey's conception of the state. My concern is with using his functional account of publics to illuminate social conflict and the proper response to such conflict. An excellent account of Dewey's view of publics and his overall account of democracy can be found in Robert B. Westbrook's *John Dewey and American Democracy* (Ithaca: Cornell University Press, 1991). Judith Green's *Deep Democracy: Community, Diversity, and Transformation* (Lanham, Md.: Rowman and Littlefield, 1999) develops pragmatism in light of contemporary discussions in democratic theory.

10. Habermas offers a worked-out account of communicative action that is similar to the notion of "communication community" that I am treating here. For an application of the idea of communicative action to moral theory see his *Moral Consciousness and Communicative Action* and *Justification and Application: Remarks on Discourse Ethics.* I agree with Habermas that democratic deliberation requires communication communities, and contemporary moral theory must interface with some conception of such democratic deliberation. However, I remain skeptical of some of the elements of his moral theory, in particular the strict separation between justifying general norms and applying them to circumstances.

11. *LW* 2:314.

12. For a discussion of publics as the products of deliberate social and political organization, see Chapter 7 of Larry Hickman's *John Dewey's Pragmatic Technology* (Bloomington: Indiana University Press, 1990).

13. James Bohman argues that we cannot rid ourselves of dependence

on experts, so the real issue becomes how to remove a pernicious deference to them, especially on matters that affect basic interests of citizens. He shows how the AIDS movement has generated activism that has helped redefine sufficient testing of experimental drugs so that these are available sooner for dying patients that wish to use them. The experts were held accountable, while at the same time required to involve the lay activist public in deliberations about epistemic criteria. See his "The Division of Labor in Democratic Discourse," in *Deliberation, Democracy, and the Media,* ed. Simone Chambers and Anne Constain, 52–55 (Lanham, Md.: Rowman and Littlefield, 2000).

14. *LW* 2:364.

15. Ibid.

16. Dewey argues this sort of point in the *Public and Its Problems* with regard to the need to better develop the news media.

17. The connection between democracy and education is something Dewey worked long and hard to understand and promote in practical and theoretical efforts.

18. James Campbell, *The Community Reconstructs: The Meaning of Pragmatic Social Thought* (Urbana: The University of Illinois Press, 1992), 63–64.

19. This section is based on a paper published in *International Philosophical Quarterly* 38, no. 1: 83–93. I would like to thank Martin Sragek, Dan Haggerty, Richard Schacht, and participants of the 1996 Syracuse Graduate Philosophy Conference for helpful comments on that paper.

20. John J. Stuhr works out a rich conception of what he calls "genealogical pragmatism." Stuhr's account of "genealogy" encompasses a conception of philosophy as cultural criticism that fits well with the approach to morality and social criticism that I endorse. My aims in linking pragmatism to genealogy in this book are more limited than Stuhr's. My focus is on demonstrating the conceptual significance of "genealogical" inquiry once one adopts a pragmatist account of moral judgment and social criticism. See the essays in *Genealogical Pragmatism: Philosophy, Experience, and Community* (Albany: State University of New York Press, 1997).

21. Couzens-Hoy makes this claim in relation to his interpretation of Nietzsche on genealogy. See his "Nietzsche, Hume, and the Genealogical Method," in *Nietzsche, Genealogy, and Morality,* ed. Richard Schacht (Berkeley: University of California Press, 1994).

22. *On the Genealogy of Morals,* trans. Walter Kaufmann (New York: Vintage Books, 1968), 15.

23. Ibid., 20.

24. Ibid., 79.

25. Ibid., 80.

26. See *The Use of Pleasure,* Vol. 2 of *The History of Sexuality,* trans. Robert Hurley (New York: Vintage, 1990).

27. Thus, a genealogical "diachronic" study of the development of the meanings and functions of a practice may provide valuable information for a "synchronic" study of the current meaning and function of a practice. One way of looking at the relation of these is that the diachronic, genealogical analysis of moral interpretations and practices helps to distance us from our immediate understandings of current practices so that we may become aware of possible flaws in these current understandings. For the remainder of this chapter I will confine my remarks about genealogy to its use as a tool for analyzing *current* moral interpretations of practices by helping us attain critical distance.

28. A number of positions could be taken here. We might hold that that the practices connected to "discourses" about insanity do not help alleviate mental disease. But we might make a second, more radical claim, that in some sense these practices "cause" or "create" the psychological condition of "insanity." It is not always clear, for example, how strong a claim Foucault wishes to make in this connection. See *The Birth of the Clinic: An Archaeology of Medical Perception,* trans. A. M. Sheridan Smith (New York: Vintage Books, 1994). Foucault's work is commonly divided up into an early "archaeological period," followed by his "genealogical writing." For my purposes here, whatever differences there are between these periods matters less than the very fundamental point that Foucault's writing as a whole seems to be concerned with debunking current normative understandings by careful historical analysis.

29. In short, I recommend that the genealogist follow the pragmatic view of inquiry as prompted by a doubt that is justified and terminated by the (at least temporary) resolution of the problematic situation that prompts such doubt.

30. Addams' account of charity is given in the second chapter, "Charitable Effort," of *Democracy and Social Ethics,* ed. Anne Firor Scott (1902; reprint, Cambridge: Belknap Press of Harvard University Press, 1964).

31. See *Animal Liberation* (New York: New York Review of Books, distributed by Random House, 1990).
32. See *The Case for Animal Rights* (Berkeley: University of California Press, 1983).
33. For a compact version of such an analysis see *Animal Liberation,* Chapter 5.
34. For an excellent account of the ways that Darwinism unseats traditional moral views of the sanctity of human life, see James Rachels, *Created from Animals: The Moral Implications of Darwinism* (New York: Oxford University Press, 1990).
35. Rollin provides a detailed interpretation of the hidden assumptions of scientific ideology that dismisses giving animals moral status in *The Unheeded Cry: Animal Consciousness, Animal Pain, and Science* (Ames: Iowa State University Press, 1998).

Bibliography

Addams, Jane. *Democracy and Social Ethics.* Ed. Anne Firor Scott. 1902. Reprint, Cambridge: Belknap Press of Harvard University Press, 1964.

———. *Twenty Years at Hull House.* Edited by James Hurt. 1910. Reprint, Urbana: University of Illinois Press, 1990.

Anscombe, G. E. M. *Intention.* Oxford: Basil Blackwell, 1957.

Arras, John D. "Getting Down to Cases: The Revival of Casuistry in Bioethics." *Journal of Medicine and Philosophy* 16 (1991): 29–51.

Aristotle. *Nicomachean Ethics.* Translated by Terence Irwin. Indianapolis: Hackett, 1985.

Baier, Annette. *Moral Prejudices: Essays on Ethics.* Cambridge: Harvard University Press, 1994.

Bohman, James. "The Division of Labor in Democratic Discourse." In *Deliberation, Democracy, and the Media,* edited by Simone Chambers and Anne Constain. Lanham, Md.: Rowman and Littlefield, 2000.

Bourdieu, Pierre. *Distinction: A Social Critique of the Judgment of Taste.* Translated by Richard Nice. Cambridge: Harvard University Press, 1984.

———. *Outline of a Theory of Practice.* Translated by Richard Nice. Cambridge: Cambridge University Press, 1977.

Bradley, F. H. *Ethical Studies.* 2nd edition. New York: Oxford University Press, 1962.

Campbell, James. *The Community Reconstructs: The Meaning of Pragmatic Social Thought.* Urbana: University of Illinois Press, 1992.

Card, Claudia. *The Unnatural Lottery: Character and Moral Luck.* Philadelphia: Temple University Press, 1996.

Dancy, Jonathon. "Ethical Particularism and Morally Relevant Properties." *Mind* 92 (1983): 530–47.

Davidson, Donald. *Essays on Actions and Events.* New York: Oxford University Press, 1980.

――――. *Inquiries into Truth and Interpretation.* New York: Oxford University Press, 1984.

Dewey, John. *The Later Works, 1925–1953.* 17 volumes. Edited by Jo Ann Boydston. Carbondale: Southern Illinois University Press; London : Feffer and Simons, 1981–1990.

――――. *The Middle Works: 1899–1924.* 15 volumes. Edited by Jo Ann Boydston. Carbondale: Southern Illinois University Press, 1976–1983.

Dworkin, Ronald. *Law's Empire.* Cambridge: Belknap Press of Harvard University Press, 1986.

Eldridge, Michael. *Transforming Experience: John Dewey's Cultural Instrumentalism.* Nashville: Vanderbilt University Press, 1998.

Flanagan, Owen J. *Varieties of Moral Personality: Ethics and Psychological Realism.* Cambridge: Harvard University Press, 1991.

Foucault, Michel. *The Birth of the Clinic: An Archaeology of Medical Perception.* Translated by A. M. Sheridan Smith. New York: Pantheon, 1973. Reprint, New York: Vintage, 1975, 1994.

――――. *The Use of Pleasure.* Vol. 2 of *The History of Sexuality.* Translated by Robert Hurley. New York: Vintage, 1990.

Green, Judith M. *Deep Democracy: Community, Diversity, and Transformation.* Lanham, Md.: Rowman and Littlefield, 1999.

Habermas, Jürgen. *Justification and Application: Remarks on Discourse Ethics.* Translated by Ciaran P. Cronin. Cambridge: MIT Press, 1993.

――――. *Moral Consciousness and Communicative Action.* Translated by Christian Lenhardt and Shierry Weber Nicholsen. Cambridge: MIT Press, 1990.

Hare, R. M. *Freedom and Reason.* Oxford: Clarendon Press, 1963.

Hickman, Larry A. *John Dewey's Pragmatic Technology.* Bloomington: Indiana University Press, 1990.

Hume, David. *An Enquiry Concerning the Principles of Morals.* Edited by J. B. Schneewind. Indianapolis: Hackett, 1983.

Johnson, Albert R., and Stephen Toulmin. *The Abuse of Casuistry: A History of Moral Reasoning.* Berkeley: University of California Press, 1988.

Johnson, Mark. *Moral Imagination: Implications of Cognitive Science for Ethics.* Chicago: The University of Chicago Press, 1993.

Kant, Immanuel. *Critique of Judgment.* Translated by Werner S. Pluhar. Indianapolis: Hackett, 1987.

————. *Grounding for the Metaphysics of Morals*. 3rd ed. Translated by James W. Ellington. Indianapolis: Hackett, 1993.

LaFollette, Hugh. "Pragmatic Ethics." In *The Blackwell Guide to Ethical Theory,* edited by Hugh LaFollette. Malden, Mass.: Blackwell, 2000.

Lekan, Todd. "The Normative Force of Genealogy in Ethics." *International Philosophical Quarterly* 38, no. 1 (1997): 83–93.

Light, Andrew, and Eric Katz. *Environmental Pragmatism*. London: Routledge, 1996.

MacIntyre, Alasdair C. *After Virtue*. 2nd ed. Notre Dame: University of Notre Dame Press, 1984.

Mackie, John L. *Ethics: Inventing Right and Wrong*. Harmondsworth, N.Y.: Penguin, 1977.

McDowell, John. "Non-Cognitivism and Rule-Following." In *Wittgenstein: To Follow a Rule,* edited by Steven H. Holtzman and Christopher M. Leich. London: Routledge and Kegan Paul, 1981.

McGee, Glen. *The Perfect Baby: A Pragmatic Approach to Genetics*. Lanham, Md.: Rowman and Littlefied, 1997.

Mead, George H. *Mind, Self, and Society*. Edited by Charles W. Morris. Chicago: University of Chicago Press, 1934; reprint, 1962.

Mill, John Stuart. *Utilitarianism*. Edited by George Sher. Indianapolis: Hackett, 1979; reprint, 1986.

Moore, G. E. *Principia Ethica*. Cambridge: Cambridge University Press, 1993.

Murphy, Arthur Edward. *The Theory of Practical Reason*. Edited by A. I. Melden. La Salle, Ill.: Open Court, 1964.

Nagel, Thomas. *The View from Nowhere*. New York: Oxford University Press, 1986.

Nietzsche, Friedrich. *On the Genealogy of Morals*. Translated by Walter Kaufmann and R. J. Hollingdale. Edited by Walter Kaufmann. New York: Vintage, 1968.

Nussbaum, Martha Craven. *Love's Knowledge: Essays on Philosophy and Literature*. New York: Oxford University Press, 1990.

O'Neill, Onora. *Constructions of Reason: Explorations of Kant's Practical Philosophy*. New York: Cambridge University Press, 1989.

Pappas, Gregory. "Dewey's Ethics: Morality as Experience." In *Reading Dewey: Interpretations for A Postmodern Generation,* edited by Larry A. Hickman. Bloomington: Indiana University Press, 1998.

Putnam, Hilary. *Words and Life*. Edited by James Conant. Cambridge: Harvard University Press, 1994.

Rachels, James. *Created from Animals: The Moral Implications of Darwinism.* New York: Oxford University Press, 1990.

Rasmussen, David. *Universalism versus Communitarianism: Contemporary Debates in Ethics.* Cambridge: MIT Press, 1990.

Rawls, John. *A Theory of Justice.* Cambridge: Belknap Press of Harvard University Press, 1971.

Regan, Tom. *The Case for Animal Rights.* Berkeley: University of California Press, 1983.

Richardson, Henry. "Truth and Ends in Dewey's Pragmatism." In *Pragmatism,* vol. 24 of *Canadian Journal of Philosophy,* edited by Cheryl Misak. Calgary: University of Calgary Press, 1999.

Rollin, Bernard E. *The Unheeded Cry: Animal Consciousness, Animal Pain, and Science.* New York : Oxford University Press, 1989. Reprint, Ames: Iowa State University Press, 1998.

Rorty, Richard. *Contingency, Irony, and Solidarity.* New York: Cambridge University Press, 1989.

———. *Objectivity, Relativism, and Truth.* New York: Cambridge University Press, 1991.

Ross, W. D. *The Right and the Good.* Oxford: Clarendon Press, 1930.

Scanlon, Thomas M. *What We Owe to Each Other.* Cambridge: Belknap Press of Harvard University Press, 1998.

Schacht, Richard, ed. *Nietzsche, Genealogy, Morality: Essays on Nietzsche's Genealogy of Morals.* Berkeley: University of California Press, 1994.

Scheffler, Samuel, ed. *Consequentialism and Its Critics.* New York: Oxford University Press, 1988.

Searle, John R. *Intentionality: An Essay in the Philosophy of Mind.* New York: Cambridge University Press, 1983.

Singer, Peter. *Animal Liberation.* New York: New York Review of Books, distributed by Random House, 1990.

Stuhr, John J. *Genealogical Pragmatism: Philosophy, Experience, and Community.* Albany: State University of New York Press, 1997.

Toulmin, Stephen. *The Uses of Argument.* Cambridge: Cambridge University Press, 1958; reprint 1964.

Veatch, Robert M. *Case Studies in Medical Ethics.* Cambridge: Harvard University Press, 1977.

Wallace, Gerald, and A. D. M. Walker, eds. *The Definition of Morality.* London: Methuen and Co., 1970.

Wallace, James D. *Ethical Norms, Particular Cases.* Ithaca: Cornell University Press, 1996.

————. *Moral Relevance and Moral Conflict.* Ithaca: Cornell University Press, 1988.

Walzer, Michael. *Interpretation and Social Criticism.* Cambridge: Harvard University Press, 1987.

————. *Spheres of Justice: A Defense of Pluralism and Equality.* New York: Basic Books, 1983.

Welchman, Jennifer. *Dewey's Ethical Thought.* Ithaca: Cornell University Press, 1995.

Westbrook, Robert B. *John Dewey and American Democracy.* Ithaca: Cornell University Press, 1991.

Westphal, Kenneth R., ed. *Pragmatism, Reason, and Norms: A Realistic Assessment.* New York: Fordham University Press, 1998.

Will, Frederick L. *Beyond Deduction: Ampliative Aspects of Philosophical Reflection.* New York: Routledge, 1988.

————. *Pragmatism and Realism.* Edited by Kenneth R. Westphal. Lanham, Md.: Rowman and Littlefield, 1997.

Williams, Bernard. *Ethics and the Limits of Philosophy.* Cambridge: Harvard University Press, 1985.

————. *Moral Luck: Philosophical Papers, 1973–1980.* New York: Cambridge University Press, 1981.

Index

action: based on practical reasoning, 15; explanation of, 178; intentional, 15, 24, 25, 178, 180; justification of contrasted with explanation of, 18

action plan, 33, 38–40, 44, 46, 49, 88, 112, 113, 140, 158

Addams, Jane, 42, 53, 54, 58, 136, 181, 182; a semi-fictional example, 47–48; as an example of pragmatist practical reasoning, 33–35, 37, 39–41, 43, 45, 46; fixed-end interpretation of, 36; on charity, 170–72

agent-relative morality, 16

Anscombe, G.E.M., 17

Aristotle, 19–20, 103, 185; on perception of the particular, 80

Arras, John D, 120

Baier, Annette, 187

Bohman, James, 191–92

Bourdieu, Pierre, 180

Bradley, F. H, 189

Campbell, James, 161–62

Card, Claudia, 187

casuistry, 104–6; as radical particularism, 103

character: as interpenetrating habits, 60; narrative structure of, 60

complexity, 22

conscience: craft contrasted with moral, 136; Dewey on, 87

consequentialism, 16

Cooper, Neil, 187

Couzens-Hoy, David, 163, 192

Dancy, Jonathon, 96–98, 103, 109; criticism of, 101; on radical particularism, 96–99, 101; on residual effects of moral principles, 99

Darwin, Charles, 145, 146, 173–74

Davidson, Donald, 179; on conceptual schemes, 191

decision problem, 111, 113, 115, 131, 137, 144; relation to ideological distortions, 114

deliberation: *see* deliberative event

deliberative event, 40, 42, 44–46, 49–50, 77, 86, 88, 89, 96, 104, 112–14, 150, 158, 163, 170, 175;